Applications Exercises Using Lotus 1-2-3 2.0, dBase III Plus, and WordStar

Alex Neely, C.S.C. Company, Spokane, Washington

Donald Barker, Gonzaga University

Chia-Ling Barker, Whitworth College

Merrill Publishing Company
A Bell & Howell Information Company
Columbus   Toronto   London   Melbourne

Published by Merrill Publishing Company
A Bell & Howell Information Company
Columbus, Ohio 43216

Administrative Editor: Vernon Anthony
Production Coordinator: Jo Ellen Gohr
Art Coordinator: Pete Robison

International Standard Book Number : 0-675-20844-0
Printed in the United States of America
1 2 3 4 5 6 7 8 9 - 90 89 88 87

PREFACE

The purpose of this workbook is to provide an opportunity
for those learning Lotus 1-2-3, dBase III Plus, and WordStar
3.3 to become more proficient in using these programs to
develop solutions to typical business computing problems.
Since this workbook is designed to be used in conjunction
with a "how to" manual, little attempt is made at explaining
basic commands. Where advanced commands are concerned,
brief explanations are provided.

Each case problem is rated for level of difficulty. The
scale ranges from 1 to 3, with 3 being the most difficult
level. The exercises for Lotus and dBase are labeled for
type of applications (i.e., Marketing, Accounting, Finance
etc.). To further aid the instructor in exercise
assignments, all problems contain a list of commands used in
solving the particular exercise.

Special thanks is given to Marlyn Fode, C.P.S., Trudie
Mischke, and Carol Wilder for their assistance and
dedication in editing and testing the exercises in this
workbook.

SECTION 3 WORDSTAR

Contents

Exercise 1

Creating Forms

Level of Difficulty: [1]

Type of Application: General

Commands Used:

> /**W**orksheet Column-Width **S**et
> /**F**ile **S**ave
> /**C**opy
> /**P**rint

Functions Used:

> None

Techniques Used:

> Using the label alignment prefixes
>
> Creating business forms
>
> Copying text ranges

Special Keys:

> [Home]   [Tab]

PROBLEM

You have been assigned to design a new employment application, an inventory count sheet and an employee expense reimbursement form. Half an hour and several sheets of paper later, you decide to use your spreadsheet to design the forms.

ANALYSIS

Both Lotus 1-2-3 and VP-Planner have the capability to function as limited text editors and store a fair amount of text, so you decide to use one worksheet file to store all of your forms.

DESIGN

The old employment application was two pages long and the new one will be approximately the same length. The inventory count sheet will be one page, and the employee expense reimbursement form will be one-half page long. To accommodate the different column widths, you elect to place the three forms side by side. This will allow the use of the tab key to move from one form to another.

DEVELOPMENT

Part A - Employment Application

1. Start with a blank worksheet, move the cell pointer to cell A1, and set the width for columns A and B to 72. (/Worksheet Column-Width Set 72 <RET>)

2. Center the following entries by preceding them with the carat (^).

    Cell
     A1   Acme Wholesale Company
     A2   Application For Employment

3. Using the repeating label indicator (\) and the "*", create a form divider in cell A3.
(* <RET>)

4. In cell A4, enter:

Last Name:[Underscore 21][Space]First Name:[Underscore 29].

(Note: Type Last Name followed by 21 underscores and a space, then type First Name followed by 29 underscores.)

5. Using the repeating label indicator (\) and the centering label indicator (^), duplicate page 1 of the employment application shown in FIGURE 1.1 on page 7.

6. Press [Home], then [Tab] to position the screen with cell B1 in the upper left corner.

Duplicate page two of the employment application as shown in FIGURE 1.2 on page 8.

7. Save file as EX1.
(/File Save EX1 <RET>)

Part B - Employee Expense Reimbursement Form

1. Move cell pointer to cell A1 by pressing [Home].

2. Press [Tab] to move one screen to the right.

3. Make the following label entries:

<u>Cell</u>   <u>Content</u>
E1   [Space 3]Employee Expense Reimbursement
(Note: Press space 3 times, then type <u>Employee Expense</u>
<u>Reimbursement</u>.)

C3   Employee:[Underscore 24]
(Note: Type <u>Employee</u>, then press underscore 24 times.)

G3   Dept:[Underscore 10]
I3   Date:[Underscore 13]
C4   \-

4. Copy cell C4 to cells D4..J4.
(**/C**opy {from} **C4..C4** <RET> {to} **D4..J4** <RET>)

5. Make the following entries:
(Note: Precede the | with an apostrophe.)

<u>Cell</u>   <u>Content</u>
C5   Item #
D5 | Description
H5 | Chg To
I5 | Amount
C6   \-
D6 |--------
E6   \-
F6   \-
G6   \-
H6 |--------
I6 |--------
J6   \-
C7   _
D7 |_____
E7   _
F7   _
G7   _
H7 |_____
I7 |_____
J7   _

6. Left align the following entries by preceding them with
an apostrophe.

<u>Cell</u>   <u>Content</u>
D8 |
H8 |
I8 |

7. Copy cells C7..J8 to cells C9..J10.
(/Copy {from} **C7..J8** <RET> {to} **C9..C9** <RET>)

Note: When copying a row of cells, it is only necessary to specify the starting cell of the destination row and the entire contents of the source row are copied to the destination row.

8. Copy cells C7..J10 to cells C11..J14.
(/Copy {from} **C7..J10** <RET> {to} **C11..C11** <RET>)

9. Copy cells C7..J14 to cells C15..J21.
(/Copy {from} **C7..J14** <RET> {to} **C15..C15** <RET>)

10. Copy cell C21..J21 to cells C23..J23.
(/Copy {from} **C21..J21** <RET> {to} **C23..C23** <RET>)

11. Make the remaining entries to complete the form as shown in FIGURE 1.3 on page 9.

12. Save the file.
(/**F**ile **S**ave **R**eplace)

Part C - Inventory Count Sheet

1. Position the screen so that cell K1 is in the upper left corner.

2. Set the following column widths:

Column	Width
L	1
P	1
Q	7
R	1
S	7
T	1
U	8
V	1

3. Make the following entries:

Cell	Content
O1	Acme Wholesale Company
N2	[Space 3]Inventory Sheet
K3	\-

4. Copy cell K3 to cells L3..W3.
(/Copy {from} **K3..K3** <RET> {to} **L3..W3** <RET>)

5. Copy cell K3..W3 to K5..W5.
(/Copy {from} **K3..W3** <RET> {to} **K5..K5** <RET>)

6. Make the following entries:
(Note: Precede the | with an apostrophe.)

<u>Cell</u>	<u>Content</u>	
K4	Date:[Underscore 12]	
N4	Dept:[Underscore 12]	
Q4	Counted By:[Underscore 23]	
K6	Stock #	
L6	|	
M6	Description	
P6	|	
Q6	Bin	(Center by preceding with ^)
R6	|	
S6	Pr	(Center by preceding with ^)
T6	|	
U6	Count	(Center by preceding with ^)
V6	|	
W6	Ext	(Right align by preceding with ")
K7	\-	
L7	|	
M7	\-	
N7	\-	
O7	\-	
P7	|	
Q7	\-	
R7	|	
S7	\-	
T7	|	
U7	\-	
V7	|	
W7	\-	
L8	|	
P8	|	
R8	|	
T8	|	
V8	|	

7. Copy cells K7..W8 to cells K9..W10.
(**/C**opy {from} **K7..W8** <RET> {to} **K9..K9** <RET>)

8. Copy cells K7..W10 to cells K11..W14.
(**/C**opy {from} **K7..W10** <RET> {to} **K11..K11** <RET>)

9. Copy cells K7..W14 to cells K15..W22.
(**/C**opy {from} **K7..W14** <RET> {to} **K15..K15** <RET>)

10. Copy cells K7..W22 to cells K23..W38.
(**/C**opy {from} **K7..W22** <RET> {to} **K23..K23** <RET>)

11. Copy cells K7..W18 to cells K39..W50.
(**/C**opy {from} **K7..W18** <RET> {to} **K39..K39** <RET>)

12. Fill cell K51 with a dashed line.
(\- <RET>)

13 Copy cell K51 to cells L51..W51.
(/Copy {from} **K51..K51** <RET> {to} **L51..W51** <RET>)

14. Complete the form as shown in FIGURE 1.4 on page 10.

15. Save the file.
(/**F**ile **S**ave **R**eplace)

Part D - One Step Beyond

Print the forms. If you can determine the proper set up
string, set the printer for 12 characters per inch.
If you are using Lotus 1-2-3, set the top and bottom margins
to 0.

Acme Wholesale Company
Application For Employment
****
Last Name:_____ First Name:_____

Address:_____

City:_____ State:_____ Zip:_____ Phone:( )___-_____

Marital Status:_____ Number of Dependents:_____

Position Applied For:_____Full-time/Part-time:_____

Date of Application_____ Salary Requirements:_____ Per:_____

Are you willing to: Relocate?_____ Work Nights?_____Week-ends?_____

****
Work History
List previous employment starting with most recent.

Employer:_____ Supervisor:_____

Address:_____

City:_____ State:_____ Zip:_____Phone:( )___-_____

From:_____ To:_____ Position:_____ Salary:_____

Responsibilities:_____

Reason for leaving:_____
~~~~~~
Employer:_____ Supervisor:_____

Address:_____

City:_____ State:_____ Zip:_____Phone:( )___-_____

From:_____ To:_____ Position:_____ Salary:_____

Responsibilities:_____

Reason for leaving:_____

****

FIGURE 1.1

Acme Wholesale Company
Application For Employment
****
Education History
Start with most recent

College or University

Name:_____ From:_____To:_____

Address:_____

Major:_____Minor:_____

Additional Studies:_____

Graduated? (Y/N)_____ Degree:_____ Credit Hrs:_____ GPA:_____
~~~~~~
Name:_____ From:_____To:_____

Address:_____

Major:_____Minor:_____

Additional Studies:_____

Graduated? (Y/N)_____ Degree:_____ Credit Hrs:_____ GPA:_____
~~~~~~
High School

Name:_____ From:_____To:_____

Address:_____

Curriculum Focus:_____

Additional Studies:_____

Graduated? (Y/N)_____Class Ranking:_____ GPA:_____
****
References
(Non-Related)
Name:_____ Years Acquainted:_____

Address:_____ Occupation:_____

City:_____State:_____ Zip:_____ Phone:(   )____-_____
~~~~~~
Name:_____ Years Acquainted:_____

Address:_____ Occupation:_____

City:_____State:_____ Zip:_____ Phone:(   )____-_____

****

FIGURE 1.2

Employee Expense Reimbursement

Employee:_____ Dept:_____ Date:_____

Item #	Description	Chg To	Amount

Employee Signature:_____ Total: _____

Approved By:_____

Date Approved:_____ Check #_____ Amount: _____

Balance: _____

FIGURE 1.3

Acme Wholesale Company
Inventory Sheet

Date:_____ Dept:_____ Counted By:_____

Stock #	Description	Bin	Pr	Count	Ext

Extended By:_____ Date:_____ Sheet Total:_____

Checked By:_____ Date:_____ Corrected Amt:_____

FIGURE 1.4

EXERCISE 2

Simple Math Demonstration

Level of Difficulty: [1]

Type of Application: General

Commands Used:

    /Copy
    /Worksheet Column-Width Set
    /File Save

Functions Used:
    None

Techniques Used:

    Changing values to labels

    Using the label prefix indicators to control alignment

    Entering values and simple formulas

Special Keys Used:

    [F5] [Tab] [PgUp] [PgDn]

PROBLEM

You work for a small manufacturing company. You just found
out that your boss's grandchildren are coming to the plant
for a visit this afternoon and he wants you to show them how
a computer works. They are seven and nine years old, so you
have to keep it simple.

ANALYSIS

You have a simple word processor that you can let them type
letters with, but you want to show them something about
spreadsheets, your forte. After spending several minutes
thinking about all of the complex spreadsheets you have
developed, you finally decide to create a simple worksheet
to show them how simple math is performed.

DESIGN

To keep things from being confusing, you decide to create
one screen illustrating each of the following:

        Addition
        Subtraction
        Multiplication
        Division
        Exponentiation
        Order of Precedence

You further decide to build the screens so that they can be easily experimented with.

DEVELOPMENT

<u>Part A - Calculator Demonstration</u>

1. Start with a clear worksheet and make the following label entries:

Cell	Content
C1	Spreadsheet Math Demonstration
A3	Calculator
A5	Move the cell pointer to cell D15.
B7	1. Type:

(Note: Precede the 1 in cell B7 with an apostrophe to convert it to a label. Do the same for cells B8..B11.)

C7	5+5

(Note: Precede the numbers in cells C7..C11 with an apostrophe to convert them to labels.)

Cell	Content	
F7	Then press <RET>	
B8	2. Type:	
C8	20-6	
B9	3. Type:	
C9	5*7	
B10	4. Type:	
C10	56/8	
B11	5. Type:	
C11	5^3	
D14	\-	
C15	|	(Precede with " to right align)
E15	|	(Precede with ' to left align)
D16	\-	
A 20	To go to the next screen, press [PgDn].	

2. Copy cell F7 to cells F8..F11.
(**/C**opy {from} **F7..F7** <RET> {to} **F8..F11** <RET>)

3. **Check your screen with FIGURE 2.1 on page 17.**

Part B - Addition Demonstration

1. Copy cell C1 to cell C21.
(**/C**opy {from} **C1..C1** <RET> {to} **C21..C21** <RET>)

2. Make the following label entries:

Cell	Content
A22	Addition
B24	1. Adding two numbers.
B26	Enter 1st number------->
B27	Enter 2nd number-------> +
E28	\-
B29	Answer---------------->
B31	2. Adding three numbers.
B33	Enter 1st number------->
B34	Enter 2nd number-------> +
B35	Enter 3rd number-------> +
E36	\-
B37	Answer---------------->
A40	To go to the next screen, press [PgDn].

3. Enter the following values and formulas:

Cell	Content
E26	6
E27	3
E29	+E26+E27
E33	15
E34	27
E35	35
E37	+E33+E34+E35

4. Check your screen with FIGURE 2.2 on page 17.

Part C - Subtraction Demonstration

1. Copy cell C21 to cell C41.
(**/C**opy {from} **C21..C21** <RET> {to} **C41..C41** <RET>)

2. Make the following label entries:

Cell	Content
A42	Subtraction
B44	1. Subtracting two numbers.
B46	Enter 1st number------->
B47	Enter 2nd number-------> -
E48	\-
B49	Answer---------------->
B51	2. Subtracting three numbers.
B53	Enter 1st number------->

```
B54        Enter 2nd number------->  -
B55        Enter 3rd number------->  -
E56        \-
B57        Answer----------------->
A60        To go to the next screen, press [PgDn].
```

3. Enter the following values and formulas:

Cell	Content
E46	9
E47	5
E49	+E46-E47
E53	124
E54	14
E55	45
E57	+E53-E54-E55

4. Check your screen with FIGURE 2.3 on page 19.

Part D - Multiplication Demonstration

1. Copy cell C41 to cell C61.
(/Copy {from} **C41..C41** <RET> {to} **C61..C61** <RET>)

2. Make the following label entries (See FIGURE 2.4 on page 18.):

```
Cell       Content
A62        Multiplication
B64        1. Multiplying two numbers.
B66        Enter 1st number------->
B67        Enter 2nd number------->  *
E68        \-
B69        Answer----------------->
B71        2. Multiplying three numbers.
B73        Enter 1st number------->
B74        Enter 2nd number------->  *
B75        Enter 3rd number------->  *
E76        \-
B77        Answer----------------->
A80        To go to the next, press [F5],type I1, and
           press <RET>.
```

3. Enter the following values and formulas:

Cell	Content
E66	9
E67	5
E69	+E66*E67
E73	5
E74	7
E75	2
E77	+E73*E74*E75

4. Check your screen with FIGURE 2.4 on page 18.

4. Check your screen with FIGURE 2.4 on page 18.

Part E - Division Demonstration

1. Set the following column widths:
(/**W**orksheet **C**olumn-Width **S**et 1 <RET>)

Column	Width
I	5
N	1
O	4
P	2
Q	5
R	2
S	8

2. Copy cell C1 to cell L1.
(/**C**opy {from} **C1..C1** <RET> {to} **L1..L1** <RET>)

3. Position the screen so that cell I1 is in the upper left corner.

4. Make the following label entries:

Cell	Content
I2	Division
J4	1. Dividing two numbers.
N6	/
P6	=

(Note: Precede / and = with ' to convert to labels.)

Cell	Content
J7	Enter 1st number[Dash 17]^[Space 5]^[Space5]^

(Note: Type <u>Enter 1st number</u>, then press [Dash] 17 times followed by ^, [Space] 5 times, ^. See FIGURE 2.5 on page 19.

Cell	Content
J8	Enter 2nd number[Dash 23]^[Space 5]^
J9	Answer[Dash 39]^
J11	2. Dividing three numbers.
N13	/
P13	/
R13	=
J14	Enter 1st number[Dash 17]^[Space 6]^[Space 6]^[Space 6]^
J15	Enter 2nd number[Dash 23]^[Space 6]^[Space 6]^
J16	Enter 3rd number[Dash 30]^[Space 6]^
J17	Answer[Dash 47]^
I20	To go to the next screen, press [PgDn].

5. Enter the following values and formulas:

Cell	Content
M6	124
O6	6
Q6	+M6/O6
M13	365
O13	7
Q13	6
S13	+M13/O13/Q13

6. Check your screen with FIGURE 2.5 on page 19.

Part F - Order of Precedence Demonstration

1. Copy cell L1 to cell L21.
(/**C**opy {from} **L1..L1** <RET> {to} **L21..L21** <RET>)

2. Make the following label entries:

Cell	Content
I22	Order of Precedence
J24	1. Natural Order
J25	Move the cell pointer to cell S30 and type the following formula:
J28	4+7-5*8/2^2
S29	\-
R30	| (Precede with " right align.)
T30	| (Precede with ' to left align.)
S31	\-
J33	2. Changing the order with parenthesis.
J34	Move the cell pointer to cell S39 and enter the following formula:
J37	4+(7-5)*(8/2)^2
S38	\-
R39	| (Precede with " to right align.)
T39	| (Precede with ' to left align.)
S40	\-
I40	To go back to the beginning, press [Home].

3. Check your screen with FIGURE 2.6 on page 19.

4. Save this file as EX2.
(/**F**ile **S**ave **EX2** <RET>)

Part G - One Step Beyond

Develop a screen to illustrate some of the simpler @ functions.

```
          A         B         C         D         E         F         G         H
 1                            Spreadsheet Math Demonstration
 2
 3    Calculator
 4
 5    Move the cell pointer to cell D15.
 6
 7                  1. Type: 5+5                    Then press <RET>
 8                  2. Type: 20-6                   Then press <RET>
 9                  3. Type: 5*7                    Then press <RET>
10                  4. Type: 56/8                   Then press <RET>
11                  5. Type: 5^3                    Then press <RET>
12
13
14                                    ---------
15                                    ¦   125  ¦
16                                    ---------
17
18
19
20    To go to the next screen, press [PgDn].
   A1


    1help 2edit 3name 4abs 5goto 6window 7data 8table 9recalculate 0graph
    408K                             12:24                              READY
```

FIGURE 2.1

```
          A         B         C         D         E         F         G         H
21                            Spreadsheet Math Demonstration
22    Addition
23
24                  1. Adding two numbers.
25
26                  Enter 1st number------->          6
27                  Enter 2nd number------->   +      3
28                                                ---------
29                  Answer----------------->          9
30
31                  2. Adding three numbers.
32
33                  Enter 1st number------->         15
34                  Enter 2nd number------->   +     27
35                  Enter 3rd number------->   +     35
36                                                ---------
37                  Answer----------------->         77
38
39
40    To go to the next screen, press [PgDn].
   A21


    1help 2edit 3name 4abs 5goto 6window 7data 8table 9recalculate 0graph
    408K                             12:25                              READY
```

FIGURE 2.2

```
          A        B         C         D         E         F         G         H
41                           Spreadsheet Math Demonstration
42  Subtraction
43
44                1. Subtracting two numbers.
45
46                Enter 1st number------->              9
47                Enter 2nd number------->    -         5
48                                                  ---------
49                Answer---------------->              4
50
51                2. Subtracting three numbers.
52
53                Enter 1st number------->            124
54                Enter 2nd number------->    -        14
55                Enter 3rd number------->    -        45
56                                                  ---------
57                Answer---------------->             65
58
59
60  To go to the next screen, press [PgDn].
   A41


    1help 2edit 3name 4abs 5goto 6window 7data 8table 9recalculate 0graph
408K                                12:01                                    READY
```

FIGURE 2.3

```
          A        B         C         D         E         F         G         H
61                           Spreadsheet Math Demonstration
62  Multiplication
63
64                1. Multiplying two numbers.
65
66                Enter 1st number------->              9
67                Enter 2nd number------->    *         5
68                                                  ---------
69                Answer---------------->             45
70
71                2. Subtracting three numbers.
72
73                Enter 1st number------->              5
74                Enter 2nd number------->    *         7
75                Enter 3rd number------->    *         2
76                                                  ---------
77                Answer---------------->             70
78
79
80  To go to the next screen, press [F5], type 11 and press <RET>.
   A61


    1help 2edit 3name 4abs 5goto 6window 7data 8table 9recalculate 0graph
408K                                12:02                                    READY
```

FIGURE 2.4

```
       I      J       K       L       M    N O P   Q R    S       T
1                        Spreadsheet Math Demonstration
2    Division
3
4         1. Dividing two numbers.
5
6                                          124 /  6 = 20.7
7         Enter 1st number-----------------^      ^       ^
8         Enter 2nd number-----------------------^       ^
9         Answer-----------------------------------------^
10
11        2. Dividing three numbers.
12
13                                         365 /  7 /    6 = 8.69048
14        Enter 1st number-----------------^      ^      ^       ^
15        Enter 2nd number-----------------------^       ^       ^
16        Enter 3rd number-----------------------------^       ^
17        Answer-----------------------------------------------^
18
19
20   To go to the next screen, press [PgDn].
  |1
```

```
   1help 2edit 3name 4abs 5goto 6window 7data 8table 9recalculate 0graph
   408K                          11:43                            READY
```

FIGURE 2.5

```
       I      J       K       L       M    N O P   Q R    S       T
21                       Spreadsheet Math Demonstration
22   Order of Precedence
23
24        1. Natural Order
25        Move the cell pointer to cell S30 and enter the following formula:
26
27
28        4+7-5*8/2^2
29                                                          --------
30                                                          :    1 :
31                                                          --------
32
33        2. Changing the order with parenthesis.
34        Move the cell pointer to cell S39 and enter the following formula:
35
36
37        4+(7-5)*(8/2)^2
38                                                          --------
39                                                          :   36 :
40   To go back to the beginning, press [Home].             --------
  |21
```

```
   1help 2edit 3name 4abs 5goto 6window 7data 8table 9recalculate 0graph
   408K                          11:44                            READY
```

FIGURE 2.6

EXERCISE 3

Earnings Statement

Level Of Difficulty: [1]

Type of application: Marketing/Accounting

Commands used:

       /Worksheet Global Column-Width
       /Worksheet Column Set
       /Worksheet Delete Column
       /Worksheet Global Format Currency
       /Worksheet Global Protection
       /Worksheet Erase Yes
       /Range Format
       /Range Label
       /Range Unprotect
       /Range Name Create
       /Copy
       /File Save
       /File Retrieve
       /Print Printer Range
       /Print Printer Options (Margins, Settings)
       /Print Printer Align
       /Print Printer Go

Functions Used:

       @SUM

Techniques Used:

       Separation of assumption and calculation
       areas

       Relative and absolute cell referencing
       Addition, subtraction, multiplication, and division

       Pointing during formula entry

       Using range names to aid in cursor movement

Special Keys:

       [F3] [F5]

PROBLEM

You have owned a small record store for the last five years. It has provided a reasonable income but you feel that you could increase the volume and profit by expanding the size of the store. While performing a feasibility study, you decide to build a worksheet to project earnings for various gross revenues based upon the performance of the business for the last five years.

ANALYSIS

An examination of the financial records reveals variable costs in the following ratios:

1. Inventory has averaged 30% of the sales revenue.
2. Annual purchases have averaged 45% of the sales revenue.
3. Salaries average $30,000 per year plus commissions of 10% of the sales revenue.
4. 5% of the sales revenue has consistently been budgeted for advertising.

In addition, the following expenses have been consistent enough to be considered constants:

1. Insurance $8,000
2. Rent............... 6,000
3. Freight............2,000
4. Telephone..........2,400
5. Office Supplies.....1,200
6. Utilities..........1,800
7. Contributions.......1,000
8. Misc. Expenses......1,200

DESIGN

Whenever practical, assumptions and data entry areas should be separated from calculation areas of the worksheet. Although it is not always possible nor practical to do so, this particular problem lends itself to this principle.

The worksheet will be comprised of two sections. The first will be used for entering sales revenue, the variable expense percentages, and the fixed expense constant amounts. Net income will also be displayed in this screen. The second section will be the actual income statement and will contain the formulas to perform the calculations. All values to be entered in the formulas will be entered automatically by referencing the appropriate values entered in the Assumptions screen.

DEVELOPMENT

Part A - Assumptions Screen

```
            A               B        C              D           E
F
1                                Earning Statement Assumptions
2
3    Sales Revenue:                        Net Income:
4
     ================================================================
5        Variable    Percent                    Fixed
6        Expenses    of Sales              Expenses     Amount
7    ------------  ---------          ----------------  ---------
8       Inventory:                              Salaries:
9       Purchases:                             Insurance:
10       Salaries:                                  Rent:
11   Advertising:                               Freight:
12                                            Telephone:
13                                      Office Supplies:
14                                            Utilities:
15                                         Contributions:
16                                      Misc. Expenses:
17
18===================================================================
```

FIGURE 3.1

1. Start with an empty worksheet and create the screen in FIGURE 3.1.

2. Set the global column width to 12.
(/Worksheet Global Column-Width **12** <RET>)

3. Move the cell pointer to column A and set the width to 14.
(/Worksheet Column Set **14** <RET>)

4. Use the repeating label prefix (\) to fill cell A4 with the double dash (=).
(\= <RET>)

5. Copy cell A4 to cells B4..F4.
(/Copy {from} **A4..A4** {to} **B4..F4** <RET>)

6. To enter the dashes in row 7, type an apostrophe followed by the number of dashes for each cell. Note: The apostrophe indicates that the dash is to be used as a label, not a minus sign.

7. To align "Office Supplies", "Contributions", and "Misc. Expenses" with the rest of the entries in the fixed expenses columns, type the entries in column C inserting the following number of spaces in front of the expense title:

```
Office Supplies  8 spaces  (7 with Lotus 1-2-3)
Contributions    10 spaces (9 with Lotus 1-2-3)
Misc. Expenses   9 spaces  (8 with Lotus 1-2-3)
```

8. Right align the cell entries from A5 to E16.
(/Range Label Right A5..E16 <RET>)
Note: If you include row 4 in the format range, the double line will be altered.

9. Globally format to , (Comma) with 0 decimal places.
(/Worksheet Global Format , 0 <RET>)

10. Format cells B8 through B11 to percentage with 0 decimal places.
(/Range Format Percent 0 <RET> **B8..B11** <RET>)

Part B - Income Statement (Report/Calculations)

1. Using [F5], or [Tab] and [PgDn], move to cell G21 and make the following entries:

Cell	Content
G21	Unicorn Sound, Inc.
G22	Projected Earnings Statement
G23	For the Year Ending June 30, 198B
G24	
G25	Sales Revenue
G26	
G27	Cost of Goods Sold
G28	
G29	Merchandise Inventory, July 1, 198A
G30	Purchases
G31	Goods Available for Sale
G32	Merchandise Inventory, June 30, 198B
G33	
G34	Cost of Goods Sold
G35	Gross Margin
G36	
G37	Expenses:
G38	Salaries
G39	Advertising
G40	Insurance
G41	Rent
G42	Freight
G43	Telephone
G44	Office Supplies
G45	Utilities
G46	Contributions

```
G47             Misc.
G48             Total Expenses
G49
G50             Net Earnings*
G51
G52             *Before depreciation & taxes
```

2. Set G column width to 41.
(/**W**orksheet **C**olumn **S**et **41** <RET>)

3. Save this worksheet as a disk file named EX3.
(/**F**ile **S**ave **EX3** <RET>)

4. Erase the screen.
(/**W**orksheet **E**rase **Y**es)

5. Retrieve file from disk.
(/**F**ile **R**etrieve **EX3** <RET>)

Part C - Enter Assumptions

1. Press [Home] to return to cell A1.

2. Enter the following values:

Cell	Value
B3	350000
B8	.30
B9	.45
B10	.10
B11	.05
E8	30000
E9	8000
E10	6000
E11	8000
E12	2400
E13	1200
E14	1800
E15	1000
E16	1200

Part D - Formula Entry

1. Range name cells A1 through F18 Assumptions.
(/**R**ange **N**ame **C**reate Assumptions <RET> **A1..F18** <RET>)

2. Range name cells G21 through K52 Inc_Stmt.
(/**R**ange **N**ame **C**reate Inc_Stmt <RET> **G21..K52** <RET>)

3. Press [**F5**] & [**F3**] and highlight **Inc_Stmt** to go to the income statement.

4. Enter the following formulas in the corresponding cells.

Cell	Formula
J25	+B3
H29	+B3*B8
H30	+B3*B9
H31	+H29+H30
H32	+B3*B8
J34	+H31-H32
J35	+J25-J34
H38	+E8+B3*B10
H39	+B3*B11
H40	+E9

5. Copy the formula in cell H40 to cells H41..H47.
(**/C**opy {from} **H40..H40** <RET> {to} **H41..H47** <RET>)

J48	@SUM(H38..H47)
J50	+J35-J48
E3	+J50

In the next four steps, notice that deleting the contents of column I causes everything to the right of column I to shift to the left one column.

6. Using [**F5**], move cursor to cell I1.

7. Press [**End**] [**Down**] to verify that column is empty.

8. Press [**End**] [**Up**] to return to cell I1.

9. Delete Column I.
(**/W**orksheet **D**elete **C**olumn **I1..I1** <RET>)

10. Format cells J38..J47 to Percent with 2 decimal places.
(**/R**ange **F**ormat **P**ercent 2 <RET> **J38..J47** <RET>)

11. Enter the following formula:

Cell	Formula
J38	+H38/$I$25

12. Copy this formula to cells J39..J47.
(**/C**opy {from range} **J38..J38** <RET> {to range} **J39..J47** <RET>)

13. Turn the global protection on.
(/**W**orksheet **G**lobal **P**rotection **E**nable)

14. Move cursor to cell B3.

15. Attempt to change the value to 450000.
(Note: You will get an error message stating that B3 is a
protected cell. Press [Esc] to return to READY mode.)

16. Unprotect cells B3, B8..B11, and E8..E16.
(/**R**ange **U**nprotect **B3..B3** <RET>)

17. Set the left margin to 0, the right margin to 80 and
print <u>Assumptions</u> by typing ASSUMPTIONS at the range prompt
from the Print menu.
(/**P**rint **P**rinter **R**ange <u>Assumptions</u> <RET> **O**ptions **M**argins
Left **0** <RET> **M**argins **R**ight **80** <RET> **Q**uit **A**lign **G**o **P**age
Quit)

18. Print <u>Inc Stmt</u> in the same manner.

19. Change the value in cell B3 to 450000 and notice the
resulting change in cell E3.

20. Reprint <u>Assumption</u> and <u>Inc Stmt</u>.

21. Save this worksheet as EX3.
(/**F**ile **S**ave **EX3** <RET> **R**eplace)

Part E - One Step Beyond

Look up the control codes in your printer manual for
condensed, enhanced, and double-strike print. For instance,
using an Epson printer, the control code for condensed print
is 015. For double strike, it is a combination of 027 and
071. Many of the control codes can be used in combinations
to create additional special effects. For instance, to
cause an Epson printer to print in near letter quality, use
a combination of enhanced and double strike. These print
control codes are specified by selecting Setup from the
Print Printer Options menu. Precede and separate
combinations of codes with a back slash (\).

EXERCISE 4

Cost Volume Profit Analysis

Level Of Difficulty: [2]

Type of Application: Accounting/Finance

Commands Used:

        /Worksheet Column Set
        /Worksheet Global Column-Width
        /Worksheet Titles Horizontal
        /Range Format
        /Range Name Create
        /Copy
        /Data Fill
        /Data Table 1
        /Graph
        /Print Options
        /File Save

Functions Used:

        @SUM

Techniques Used:

        Copying multiple cell label ranges
        Copying relative formulas
        Copying absolute formulas
        Creating easy access screens
        Basic math operations

Special Keys:
        [F3] [F5] [F8] [F9] [F10] [PgUp] [PgDn]

PROBLEM

Businesses are often faced with deciding whether or not to
manufacture or carry new product lines. One of the points
to consider in making such a decision is what sort of sales
volume is required to produce a profit.

You are considering developing and marketing a new
electronic mouse trap and want to know how many you must
sell before the endeavor becomes profitable.

ANALYSIS

In manufacturing and selling a product, you will have three basic types of costs: initial product development, fixed, and variable (costs that vary with the number of units sold).

You make the following assumptions:

Initial product development	$ 25,000

Annual Fixed Costs:

Rent	$ 12,000
Office Salaries	130,000
Insurance	50,000
Freight	8,000
Telephone	4,300
Office Supplies	1,200
Utilities	7,500
Maintenance & Repairs	5,000
Miscellaneous Expenses	3,500

Variable Costs (per unit):

Raw Materials	$ 980
Packaging	28
Labor	1,200

Variable Costs (percent of gross sales)

Sales Commissions	12 %
Advertising	2 %
Miscellaneous Variable Costs	1 %

DESIGN

Unlike the worksheet in Exercise 1, this worksheet will be more efficient if we include a few formulas in the assumption areas.

To start with, we will need to create four separate worksheet areas. The first two will calculate fixed and variable costs. The third will calculate profits based upon a specific quantity sold at a set price. The fourth will create a table showing the profits for a wide range of sales as well as the break-even point.

To make it easier to view the separate areas of the worksheet, they will be located in the same column range so that the page down [PgDn] or page up keys [PgUp] will quickly move from screen to screen. We will also give each screen a range name to make the printing process easier.

DEVELOPMENT

Part A: Worksheet Heading and Screens

1. Set the global column width to 9.
(**/W**orksheet **G**lobal **C**olumn-Width **9** <RET>)

2. Move cursor to each column listed below and set the corresponding column widths:
(**/W**orksheet **C**olumn **S**et **19** <RET>)
(Note: **/W**orksheet **C**olumn **S**et-Width for Lotus 2.0 & 2.01)

Column	Width
A	19
B	12
C	11
D	11
E	11
G	7

3. Use the repeating label prefix (\) to fill cells A1 and A4 with the tilde.
(**\~** <RET>)

4. Use the repeating label prefix to fill cell A6 with a dashed line.
(**\-** <RET>)

5. Use the Copy command to copy from the cell range **A1..A6** to the cell range **B1..E1.**
(**/C**opy {from} A1..A6 <RET> {to} B1..G1 <RET>)

6. Enter the rest of the heading and fixed cost labels as shown in FIGURES 4.1, 4.2, 4.3, & 4.4. Extend the dashed lines to column G.

```
              A              B              C              D              E
1
~~~~~~~~~~~~~~~~~~~~~~~~~~~~~~~~~~~~~~~~~~~~~~~~~~~~~~~~~~~~~~~~~~~~~~~~~~~~~~~~~~
2                                  Acme Manufacturing Company
3                               Cost-Volume-Profit Analysis Report
4~~~~~~~~~~~~~~~~~~~~~~~~~~~~~~~~~~~~~~~~~~~~~~~~~~~~~~~~~~~~~~~~~~~~~~~~~~~~~~~~~
5                               Fixed Costs - Electronic Mousetrap
6----------------------------------------------------------------------------
7
8  Development Costs
9  Rent
10 Office Salaries
11 Insurance
12 Freight
13 Telephone
14 Office Supplies
15 Utilities
16 Misc. Expenses
17                                                      -----------
18 Total Fixed Costs
```

FIGURE 4.1

```
        A                    B              C              D              E
21                        Variable Costs - Electronic Mousetrap
22 -----------------------------------------------------------------------
23
24 Unit Price
25
26 Raw Materials
27 Packaging
28 Labor
29 Sales Commission @
30 Advertising @
31 Misc. Var. Costs @
32                                     --------                    -------
33 Total Variable Costs
34                                                 --------        -------
35 Gross Profit Per Unit
36
```

FIGURE 4.2

```
        A                    B              C              D              E
37                        Projected Profits - Electronic Mousetrap
38 -----------------------------------------------------------------------
39
40 Units Sold
41 Selling Price
42
43 Total Revenue
44 Total Fixed Costs
45 Total Variable Costs
46                                     --------                    -------
47 Total Costs
48                                                 --------        -------
49 Profit (or Loss)
50
```

FIGURE 4.3

	A	B	C	D	E
			Cost-Volume	Profit Table	
53					
54			Electronic	Mousetrap	
55	Units Sold	Revenue	Costs	Profit	% Profit
56	----------	-------	--------	--------	---------
57					
58					
59					
60					
61					
62					
63					
64					
65					
66					

FIGURE 4.4

Part B: Range Name Create, Values, Formulas

1. Assign the following range name: Fixed Costs.
(/Range Name Create Fixed Costs <RET> A5..G18 <RET>)

Cell Range	Name
A5..G18	Fixed Costs
A21..G35	Variable Costs
A37..G49	Proj Profits
A53..G87	CVP Table

2. Use the [Home] key (number 7 on the number key pad) to move the cursor to the home position.

3. Move the cursor to row 5 and lock the above rows as a horizontal title.
(/Worksheet Titles Horizontal)

4. Press [PgDn] or press [F5] followed by [F3], highlight a range, and press <RET> to view the various screens.

5. Enter the following values and formula in column D in the Fixed Costs screen:

Development Costs	25000
Rent	12000
Office Salaries	130000
Insurance	50000
Freight	8000
Telephone	4300
Office Supplies	1200
Utilities	7500
Misc. Expenses	3500
Total Fixed Costs	@SUM(D8..D16)

6. Format cells D8..D18 to , (Comma) with 0 decimal places.
(/**R**ange **F**ormat **,** **0** <RET> **D8..D18** <RET>)

7. Enter the following values and formulas in the Variable
Costs screen:

Line	Column	Formula
Unit Price	D	3500
Unit Price	E	1
Raw Materials	C	980
Raw Materials	E	+C26/$D$24
Packaging	C	28
Labor	C	1200
Sales Commission	B	.12
Sales Commission	C	+B29*$D$24
Advertising	B	.02
Misc. Var. Costs	B	.01
Total Variable Costs	D	@SUM(C26..C31)
Total Variable Costs	E	+D33/$D$24
Gross Profit Per Unit	D	+D24-D33
Gross Profit Per Unit	E	+E24-E33

8. Copy cell E26 to cells E27..E31.
   (Move cursor to cell E26)
   (/**C**opy {from} **E26..E26** <RET> {to} **E27..E31** <RET>)

9. Copy cells C29 to cells C30..C31.
   (Move cursor to cell C29)
   (/**C**opy {from} **C29..C29** <RET> {to} **C30..C31** <RET>)

10. Format cells B29..B31 to percent with 0 decimal places.
(/**R**ange **F**ormat **P**ercent **0** <RET> **B29..B31** <RET>)

11. Format cells C24..D35 to , (Comma) with 0 decimals
places.
(/**R**ange **F**ormat **,** **0** <RET> **C24..D35** <RET>)

12. Format cells E24..E35 to percent with 1 decimal place.
(/**R**ange **F**ormat **P**ercent **1** <RET> **E24..E35** <RET>)

13. Move cursor to cell A21. Use either the [**F5**][**F3**]
combination or [**PgDn**] to move to the Projected Profits
screen.

14. Enter the following values or formulas:

Line	Column	Formula
Units Sold	B	316
Selling Price	B	3500
Total Revenue	D	+B40*B41
Total Revenue	E	+D43/$D$43
Total Fixed Costs	C	+D18
Total Fixed Costs	E	+C44/$D$43

Total Variable Costs	C	+D33*B40
Total Variable Costs	E	+C45/$D$43
Total Costs	D	@SUM(C44..C45)
Total Costs	E	+D47/$D$43
Profit (or loss)	D	+D43-D47
Profit (or loss)	E	+D49/$D$43

15. Format cells B40..D49 to , with 0 decimals.
(/Range Format , 0 <RET> B40..D49 <RET>)

16. Format cells E43..E49 to percent with 1 decimal place.
(/Range Format Percent 1 <RET> E43..E49 <RET>)

17. Save file as EX4.
(/File Save EX4 <RET>)

Part C: Data Table

1. Move cursor to cell A37. Use either [F5], [F3], or
[PgDn] to move to the Cost Volume Profit screen.

2. Move cursor to cell A58 and use the Data Fill command to
fill cells A58..A88 with values starting with 20 in
increments of 20 (20,40,60,80...).
(/Data Fill {Range} A58..A88 <RET> {Start} 20 <RET> {Step}
20 <RET> {Stop} 600 <RET>)

3. Enter the following formulas in row 57.

Column	Formula
B	+D43
C	+D47
D	+D49
E	+E49

4. Use the Data Table 1 command to produce the Cost Volume
Profit table.
(/Data Table 1 {Range} A57..E87 <RET> {Input Cell} B40
<RET>)

5. Format cells B57..D87 to , (Comma) with 0 decimal places.
(/Range Format , 0 <RET> B57.. D87 <RET>)

6. Format cells E57..E87 to percent with 1 decimal place.
(/Range Format Percent 1 <RET> E57..E87 <RET>)

Part D: Print

Note: Once you enter the Print menu structure, you will
remain there until you issue a Quit command from the main
Print menu. All subsequent instructions for commands to be
issued are written with the assumption that you are still at
the main Print menu.

1. Access the main Print menu.
(**/P**rint **P**rinter)

2. Clear all previous settings.
(**C**lear **A**ll)

3. Access the Options menu, set the left margin to 0 and the right margin to 80.
(**O**ptions **M**argins **L**eft **0** <RET> **M**argins **R**ight **80** <RET>)

4. While still in the Options menu set up a row border for rows A1..A4.
(**B**order **R**ow **A1..A4** <RET>)

Note: You must issue a Quit command to return to the main Print menu.

5. Return to the main Print menu.
(**Q**uit)

6. Make sure your printer is on, align the paper and print Fixed Costs range.
(**R**ange [**F3**] |highlight Fixed Costs| <RET> **A**lign **G**o)

7. Advance the paper two lines.
(**L**ine **L**ine)

8. Cancel border range.
(**C**lear **B**orders)

9. Set print range to Variable Costs and print.
(**R**ange [**F3**] |highlight Variable Costs| <RET> **G**o)
(Note: Do not re-issue Align command.)

10. Advance the paper two lines.
(**L**ine **L**ine)

11. Set print range to Proj Profits and print.
(**R**ange [**F3**] |highlight Proj Profits| <RET> **G**o)
(Note: Do not re-issue Align command.)

12. Advance paper to next top of form.
(**P**age)

13. Reset border to rows A1..A4.
(**O**ptions **B**orders **R**ows **A1..A4** <RET> **Q**uit)

14. Set print range to CVP Table, print and quit Print menu.
(**R**ange [**F3**] |highlight CVP Table| <RET> **A**lign **G**o **P**age **P**age **Q**uit)

Part E: Graph

Note: Once you enter the Graph menu structure, you will remain there until you issue a Quit command from the main Graph menu. All subsequent instructions for commands to be issued are written with the assumption that you are still at the main Graph menu.

1. Access the main Graph menu.
(**/G**raph)

2. Select line from the Type command.
(**T**ype **L**ine)

3. Set the X axis range to A58..A87, the A data range to B58..B87, and the B data range to C58..C87 and view the graph.
(**X A58..A87** <RET> **A B58..B87** <RET> **B C58..C87** <RET> **V**iew)

4. Press any key to return to the Graph menu.

5. Enter <u>Revenue</u> as the A data legend and <u>Costs</u> as the B data legend.
(**O**ptions **L**egends **A** <u>Revenue</u> <RET> **L**egends **B** <u>Costs</u> <RET>)

6. Enter the first line title as <u>COST VOLUME PROFIT ANALYSIS</u>.
(**T**itles **F**irst <u>COST</u> <u>VOLUME</u> <u>PROFIT</u> <u>ANALYSIS</u> <RET>)

7. Enter the second line title as <u>Electronic Mousetrap</u>.
(**T**itles **S**econd <u>Electronic</u> <u>Mousetrap</u> <RET>)

8. Enter the X range title as <u>Units Sold</u>.
(**T**itles **X** <u>Units</u> <u>Sold</u> <RET>)

9. Set the Y scale format to currency with 0 decimal place view the graph, and quit the Graph menu.
(**S**cale **Y**-Scale **F**ormat **C**urrency **0** <RET> **Q**uit **Q**uit **V**iew <RET> **Q**uit)

10. To view the graph from the READY mode, press [**F10**].

11. Save the file.
(**/F**ile **S**ave **R**eplace)

Part F - One Step Beyond

Create and display a third line of data representing the constant fixed costs amount. (Hint: It should be a horizontal line.)

EXERCISE 5

INVOICE SYSTEM

Level Of Difficulty: [2]

Type of Application: General

Commands Used:

       /**Worksheet S**tatus
       /**Worksheet G**lobal **C**olumn-**W**idth
       /**Worksheet C**olumn-**W**idth **S**et
       /**Range F**ormat (Date, Comma, Percent, Currency)
       /**Data S**ort
       /**C**opy
       /**P**rint

Functions Used:

       @TODAY
       @VLOOKUP
       @HLOOKUP
       @IF
       @ROUND
       @SUM

Techniques Used:

       Using look-up tables
       Conditional testing for formula execution
       Nesting @ functions
       Copying formulas with absolute ranges
       Printing cell formulas

PROBLEM

You own a small auto parts store that sells parts to large
automotive repair shops, service stations, and over-the-
counter customers. You have three different markup levels
for these customers. Sales to the repair shops are priced
at cost plus 10 percent. Sales to the service stations are
priced at cost plus 15 percent. Over-the-counter sales are
priced at cost plus 20 percent. You want an invoicing
system that will allow you to enter the part number and have
the correct sales price calculated based upon the
appropriate pricing level.

DESIGN

This particular problem will require three separate areas an the spreadsheet. First, we will need an inventory section in which to store the part numbers, descriptions, and unit costs. Second, we will need an area to list the percentage of markup for each pricing level. Third, we will need an invoice area.

Since the physical size of the spreadsheet affects the amount of memory used to some degree, (depending upon what type of memory management technique is used in the spreadsheet package that you are using) it is usually a good idea to try minimize the number of columns that are used. With this in mind, the spreadsheet will be laid out in the following manner:

```
|-----------------------------------------------------------------|
|                               |                                 |
|        Inventory Area         |          Price Level            |
|                               |            Area                 |
|                               |                                 |
|                               |---------------------------------|
|                               |                                 |
|                               |          Invoice Area           |
|                               |                                 |
|                               |                                 |
|                               |                                 |
|                               |                                 |
|                               |                                 |
```

The formulas in the invoice area will use the @LOOKUP functions to find the correct unit cost and price level and then calculate the extended price for each item based upon the number of units sold. Sales to repair shops and service stations are not subject to sales tax as the parts will be resold. Sales tax will be added to over the counter sales.

DEVELOPMENT

<u>Part A - Setting up the Worksheet</u>

1. Check the worksheet status to make sure that the global column width is set to 9.
(**/W**orksheet **S**tatus)

Note: Press any key to return to READY mode.

2. If necessary, set the global column width to 9.
(**/W**orksheet **G**lobal **C**olumn-Width **9** <RET>)

3. Set the following column widths.
(**/W**orksheet **C**olumn-Width **S**et **22** <RET>)

Column	Width
B	22
C	22
F	10
G	30

4. Create the screens shown in FIGURES 5.1 and 5.2.

5. Set the following range formats:
(/Range Format , 2 <RET> **D6..D20** <RET>)

Range	Format
D6..D20	Comma with 2 decimals
F7..F7	Date 1 (dd-mmm-yr)
H12..H20	Comma with 2 decimals
J23..J23	Percent with 1 decimal
K12..K23	Comma with 2 decimals
K25..K25	Currency with 2 decimals

6. Make the following entries:

Cell	Content
G1	Price Level
G2	% Markup
H1	1
H2	.10
I1	2
I2	.15
J1	3
J2	.20

Part B - Entering Formulas

In order for the @VLOOKUP and @HLOOKUP commands to work, the look-up tables must be sorted in ascending order with the first column in the table as the primary sort key.

1. Sort the inventory table in ascending order with column A as the Primary Key.
(/Data Sort Data-Range {Range} **A6..E20** <RET> Primary Key **A6** <RET> **A** <RET> **G**o)

	A	B	C	D	E
1			White's Auto Parts		
2			Inventory		
3	--				
4	Part#	Description	Source		Cost Unit
5	--				
6	2345	Intake Manifold	Western Distributors		125.00 Ea
7	4576	Carburetor	Western Distributors		85.00 Ea
8	3333	Spark Plugs	B & B Auto Electrical		.99 Ea
9	3334	Spark Plug Wires	Acme Wire		2.00 Ea
10	4450	Condenser	B & B Auto Electric		1.25 Ea
11	4345	Points	B & B Auto Electric		4.29 Ea
12	456	Muffler	A to Z Exhaust		27.95 Ea
13	1835	Radiator	Radiators Inc.		185.00 Ea
14	254	Gas Cap	Auto Accessories, Inc.		.95 Ea
15	657	Hub Caps	Auto Accessories, Inc.		15.00 Ea
16	5467	Brake Pads	Auto Accessories, Inc.		12.00 Ea
17	8765	Seat Covers	Western Distributing		125.00 Ea
18	8989	Auto Stereo/Cassette	Desert Auto Stereos		347.00 Ea
19	45	Liquid Wrench	Acme Chemical		1.25 Ea
20	46	Hand Cleaner	Acme Chemical		1.58 Ea

FIGURE 5.1

	F	G	H	I	J	K
1						
2						
3						
4						
5						
6	==					
7		White's Auto Parts		Invoice #		
8	==					
9	Sold To:			Code:		
10						
11						
12						
13	==					
14	Part#	Description	Unit Price		Qty	Total
15	--					
16						
17						
18						
19						
20						
21	--					
22				Subtotal		
23				Sales Tax		
24						-------
25				Total		

FIGURE 5.2

2. Enter the following formulas:

Cell	Formula
F7	@TODAY
H16	@IF(F16>0,@VLOOKUP(F16,$A$6..$D$20,3) *(1+@HLOOKUP($K$9,$H$1..$J$2,1)),0)
K16	@ROUND(H16*J16,2)
K22	@SUM(K16..K20)
J23	@IF(K9=3,.078,0)
K23	@ROUND(K22*J23,2)
K25	+K22+K23

3. Copy the formula in cells H16 and K16 to cells H17..K20 (/Copy {from} **H16..K16** <RET> **H17..H20** <RET>)

Part C - Entering Invoice Data

1. Make the following invoice entry:

Invoice # 1

Sold To: Johnson Automotive
           S 7 Main St.
           Southport, WA 99218

Code: 1

Part#	Description	Qty
2345	Intake Manifold	1
4576	Carburetor	1
3333	Spark Plugs	6
46	Hand Cleaner	1

2. Change the price level code to 2 then 3 and notice the changes in the worksheet.

3. Change the price level code back to 1.

4. Set the right margin to 80 and print the invoice.
(**/Print Printer Range F6...K25** <RET> **O**ptions **M**argins **R**ight **80**
<RET> **Q**uit **A**lign **G**o **P**age **Q**uit)

5. Make the next two entries and print each invoice.

    Invoice #2

    Sold To: John Doe
               North 34 Oak Street
               Spokane, WA 99204

    Code: 3

Part#	Description	Qty
3333	Spark Plugs	4
3334	Spark Plug Wires	4
4450	Condenser	1
4345	Points	1

    Invoice # 3

    Sold To: Smith's Service Station
               West 23 Maple
               Valley, WA 99201

    Code: 2

Part#	Description	Qty
1835	Radiator	1
5467	Brake Pads	4

6. Print the entire worksheet with the cell formulas displayed.
(**/Print Printer Range A1..K25** <RET> **O**ptions **O**ther **C**ell
Formulas **Q**uit **A**lign **G**o **P**age **Q**uit)

7. Save this worksheet as EX5.
(**/F**ile **S**ave **EX5** <RET>)

Part C - One Step Beyond

Modify the worksheet to include a customer look-up table so
that the proper price level code is automatically set by
entering a customer number. If you are using a spreadsheet
that supports string handling, include formulas to look up
the customer's name, address, and the description of the
items being sold.

EXERCISE 6

Illustrating Market Share

Level of Difficulty: [2]

Type of Application: Marketing

Commands Used:

    /Worksheet Column-Width Set
    /Copy
    /Range Format   (Comma, Percent)
    /Graph Type   (Pie, Line, Bar)
    /Graph Options   (Titles, Scale, Legend)
    /Graph Name   (Create, Use)
    /Graph Reset   (Graph, Data Ranges)
    /Graph View
    /Graph Save
    /Graph Print   (VP-Planner)
    /File Save

Functions Used:

    @SUM
    @ROUND
    @TODAY

Techniques Used:

    Developing multiple graphs from one spreadsheet

    Using the Graph Reset command to expedite creating a
    graph from an existing graph

    Printing graph from VP-Planner's Graph menu

    Printing graphs with Lotus 1-2-3's Print Graph program

Special Keys

    [F10]

PROBLEM

You are an account executive for a small advertising firm.
One of your clients, Bonger Bat Company, manufactures and
markets baseball bats. You have managed their advertising
strategies for two years and they are beginning to question
your effectiveness. You decide to gather all of your market
research data and create a series of graphs to demonstrate

the positive effect your agency has had on their sales and market share.

ANALYSIS

In 1980, one of the Bonger Bat Company's competitors, Slugger Bats, introduced a new product line and started gaining ground on the competition. Their market share went from 41.4% in 1980 to 47.7% by the end of 1984. During the same time period, Bonger fell from a 12.3% market share to 10.8%. Acme and XYZ experienced similar declines.

In January of 1985, Bonger hired your agency to try to reverse the downward trend. Although there have been no shattering miracles, Bonger's market share had increased to 11.7% by the end of 1986 and is projected to rise to 12.3% by the end of 1987.

To illustrate a quick view of the decline in market share Bonger Bat Company experienced prior to your involvement, you decide upon two pie charts. The first chart will depict the market share profile in 1980. The second will represent the market share distribution in 1984, the low ebb for Bonger and the year prior to your involvement. Following the two pie charts, you plan to show a bar graph illustrating Bonger's annual sales from 1980 through 1986 including the 1987 projections, and a line graph giving a composite view of the market share distribution from 1980 to the 1987 projections. This will be followed by one more pie chart emphasizing the 1987 market share projections which will show that through your efforts, Bonger will have recovered their original market share and a positive trend line. Finally, you plan to present a line graph showing Bonger's sales from 1980 through the 1987 projections.

DEVELOPMENT

By using the Graph Name Create command, it is possible to create several graphs for a single worksheet. You have all of the sales data for Bonger Bat and its three major competitors. All that is necessary is to create a worksheet in a database format, create the graphs from that data, and assign each graph a name. These graphs can then be saved for future printing.

Part A - Create Worksheet

1. Starting with a clear worksheet, set the following column widths:
(/Worksheet Column-Width Set 12 <RET>)

```
C                    12
D                    12
E                    12
F                    12
G                    12
H                    12
I                    12
J                    12
```

2. Make the following cell entries:

Cell	Content
C1	Acme Advertising
A3	Market data for Bonger Bat Co.
E3	Date
F3	@TODAY

3. Format cell F3 to Date 1.
(**/Range Format Date 1** <RET> **F3..F3** <RET>)

4. Use the repeating label prefix indicator (\) to fill cell A4 with a dashed line.
(**\-** <RET>)

5. Copy cell A4 to cells B4..J4.
(**/Copy** {from} **A4..A4** {to} **B4..J4** <RET>)

6. Move the cursor to cell B6, press the space bar 4 times and make the following entry:

|------------------- Annual Sales --------------------|

7. Move the cursor to cell G1 and make the following entry:

|---------------- Market Share ----------------|

8. Enter the following column headings (right aligned):

Cell	Content
B8	Bonger
C8	XYZ
D8	Ace
E8	Slugger
F8	Total
G8	Bonger
H8	XYZ
I8	Ace
J8	Slugger
A9	Year

9. Enter the following sales data:

Year	Bonger	XYZ	Ace	Slugger
1980	98000	120000	250000	330000

1981	99000	125000	255000	360000
1982	102500	132000	265000	424000
1983	105600	135500	270500	456600
1984	106800	138000	277300	472200
1985	113400	139300	277300	481000
1986	120950	143400	280400	490000
PROJ 1987	132500	148500	288500	509000

10. Enter the following formula in cell F10:

    @SUM(B10..E10)

11. Copy cell F10 to cells F11..F17.
(/Copy {from} **F10..F10** {to} **F11..F17** <RET>)

12. Format cells B10.. F17 to , (Comma) with 0 decimal places.
(/**R**ange **F**ormat , **0** <RET> **B10..F17** <RET>)

13. Enter the following formula in cell G10:

    @ROUND(B10/$F10,3)

14. Range format cell G10 to percent with 1 decimal place.
(/**R**ange **F**ormat **P**ercent **1** <RET> **G10..G10** <RET>)

To copy the formula in cell G10 to the rest of the Market Share area in one step, the "from" cell, G10, will be included in the "to" range.

15. Copy cell G10 to cells G10..J17.
(/**C**opy {from} **G10..G10** {to} **G10..J17** <RET>)

Notice that the cell format (percent with 2 decimals) is copied along with the formula.

Part B - Pie Charts

1980 Market Share

1. Press the [Home] key to move the cursor to cell A1.

2. Create a pie chart using the 1980 sales data.
(/**G**raph **T**ype **P**ie **A** **B10..E10** <RET>)

Note: The Graph command is similar to the Print command in that once you are in the Graph menus, you will remain there until Quit is pressed from the MAIN Graph menu. These are fondly referred to as "sticky menus". Several of the Graph sub-menus also require the issuance of Quit to return to the main Graph menu. Because of the "sticky nature" of the Graph menu, it is only necessary to press the command key

[/] once to issue any Graph command. You will notice that the "/" is missing from all but the /Graph Type command in step #2.

3. View the graph.
(View)

Note: Press any key to return to the main Graph menu.

4. Add first title.
(Options Titles First *Market Share* <RET>)

5. Add second title and quit Options menu.
(Titles Second *1980* <RET> Quit)

6. View the graph.
(View)

7. Assign the X range to attach meaning to the data range.
(X B8..E8 <RET>)

8. View the Graph.
(View)

9. Name this graph MkShr 1980.
(Name Create *MKSHR 1980* <RET>)

10. To expedite the creation of the next pie chart, reset the A data range.
(Reset A <RET> Quit)

This will allow the use of the previous graph setting, thus minimizing the number of changes to be made in creating the next graph.

1984 Market Share

11. Set the A range to cells B14..E14.
(A B14..E14 <RET>)

12. Change the second title line to 1984.
(Options Titles Second *1984* <RET> Quit)

13. View the graph.
(View)

14. Name this graph MkShr 1984.
(Name Create *MKSHR 1984* <RET>)

15. Reset the A range.
(Reset A <RET> Quit)

<u>1987 Projected Market Share</u>

16. Set the A range to cells B17..E17.
(**A B17..E17** <RET>)

17. Change the second line title to <u>1987 Projection</u>.
(**O**ptions **T**itles **S**econd <u>1987 Projection</u> <RET> **Q**uit)

18. View the graph.
(**V**iew)

19. Name this graph <u>MkShr 1987 Proj</u>.
(**N**ame **C**reate <u>MKSHR 1987 PROJ</u> <RET>)

20. Reset all graph settings.
(**R**eset **G**raph)

<u>Part C - Bar Graphs</u>

<u>Sales, 1980 - 1987 Projected</u>

1. Set graph type to bar graph with an A data range of B10..B17.
(**T**ype **B**ar **A B10..B17** <RET>)

2. Set X range to A10..A17.
(**X A10..A17** <RET>)

3. View the graph.
(**V**iew)

4. Set first title to <u>Bonger Bat - Sales</u>.
(**O**ptions **T**itles **F**irst <u>Bonger Bat - Sales</u> <RET>)

5. Set second title to <u>1980 - 1987 (Projected)</u>.
(**T**itles **S**econd <u>1980 - 1987 (Projected)</u> <RET>)

6. Set X-axis title to <u>Year</u>.
(**T**itles X-axis <u>Year</u> <RET>)

7. Set Y-axis title to <u>Dollars</u> and return to the main Graph menu.
(**T**itles Y-axis <u>Dollars</u> <RET> **Q**uit)

8. View the graph.
(**V**iew)

9. Change the Y-axis scale to manual with a lower limit of 60,000 and an upper limit of 180,000.
(**O**ptions **S**cale **Y**-axis **M**anual **L**ower **60000** <RET> Upper **180000** <RET>)

Note: Lotus 1-2-3 Release 2.01 may continue to display the lower limit as 0.

10. Format the Y-axis values to currency with 0 decimal places.
(**F**ormat **C**urrency **0** <RET> **Q**uit **Q**uit)

11. View the graph.
(**V**iew)

12. Name this graph Sls 80-87 Proj1.
(**N**ame **C**reate Sls 80-87 Proj1 <RET>)

13. Reset all graph settings.
(**R**eset **G**raph)

Part D - Line Graphs

Market Share 1980 - 1987 (Projected)

1. Set graph type to line.
(**T**ype **L**ine)

2. Set the following data ranges:
(**A** **G10..G17** <RET>)

Data Set	Range
A	G10..G17
B	H10..H17
C	I10..I17
D	J10..J17
X	A10..A17

3. View the graph.
(**V**iew)

4. Set the first title to Market Share.
(**O**ptions **T**itles **F**irst Market Share <RET>)

5. Set the second title to 1980 - 1987 (Projected).
(**T**itles **S**econd 1980 - 1987 (Projected) <RET>)

6. Set the X-axis title to Year.
(**T**itles **X**-axis Year <RET>)

7. Set the Y-axis title to Percent.
(**T**itles **Y**-axis Percent <RET>)

8. Set the following legends:
(**L**egends **A** Bonger <RET>)

Data Range	Legend
A	Bonger
B	XYZ
C	Ace
D	Slugger

9. Set the Y-axis format to percent with 0 decimal places.
(**S**cale **Y**-axis **F**ormat **P**ercent **0** <RET>)

10. Quit the Options menu and view the graph.
(**Q**uit **Q**uit **V**iew)

11. Name this graph <u>MkShr 80-87 Proj</u>.
(**N**ame **C**reate <u>MkShr 80-87 Proj</u> <RET>)

12. Reset graph settings.
(Reset Graph)

Sales, 1980 - 1987 Projected - Line Graph

The bar graph depicting Bonger's sales from 1980 through the 1987 projections can be modified and changed to a line graph to leave the management with a more impressive image of the effectiveness you agency has had in influencing Bonger's sales.

1. Recall the bar graph named <u>Sls 80-87 Proj1</u>.
(**N**ame **U**se |highlight <u>Sls 80-87 Proj1</u>| <RET>)

2. Change the graph type to line.
(**T**ype **L**ine)

3. Change the Y-axis scale to automatic.
(Options **S**cale **Y**-axis **A**utomatic **Q**uit)

4. Quit the Options menu and view the graph.
(**Q**uit **V**iew)

5. Name this graph <u>Sls 80-87 Proj2</u>.
(**N**ame **C**reate <u>Sls 80-87 Proj2</u> <RET>)

6. Quit the Graph menu and save the worksheet as EX6.
(**Q**uit /**F**ile **S**ave EX6 <RET>)

Part E - Displaying the Graphs

Saving the worksheet saves all of the graphs created and named. To view any of these graphs, it is only necessary to retrieve the worksheet file and select the graphs to be viewed from the Graph Name Use command.

1. If you exited the program after Part D, retrieve the worksheet file named EX6.

2. View the MkShr 1980 pie chart.
(/Graph Name Use |highlight MkShr 1980| <RET>)

3. Using Name Use, view the remaining graphs.

Part F - Printing Graphs

Printing graphs depends upon which spreadsheet package you are using. With VP-Planner version 1.3, graphs can be printed directly from the main Graph menu. With Lotus 1-2-3 (all versions) it is necessary to save the graph with the Save selection from the main Graph menu, exit 1-2-3, and use the Lotus Print Graph program to produce the print-out.

This sections is divided into two parts. One for VP-Planner, the other for Lotus 1-2-3.

VP Planner

To print the graphs created for the Bonger presentation, it is only necessary to select the graph to be printed with the Name Use command, then select the Print command from the main Graph menu.

1. Enter the main Graph menu and select MKSHR 1980.
(/Graph Name Use |highlight MKSHR 1980| <RET>)

Remember - press any key to return to the Graph menu.

2. Make sure printer is ready and print graph.
(Print)

3. Select and print the next graph.
(Name Use |highlight MKSHR 1984| <RET> Print)

4. Print the remaining graphs.

You may also save each graph as a special graph file using the Save selection from the main Graph menu. This will create a disk file with a file extension of PIC rather than the normal worksheet extension of WKS. These files may then be used by the Lotus 1-2-3 print graph program or any of the graph enhancement packages that read Lotus 1-2-3 graph (PIC) files.

Lotus 1-2-3

Some computer systems, such as the AT&T 6300, have the capability of printing Lotus 1-2-3 graphs simply by doing a print screen (pressing [Shift] and [PrtSc] at the same time). In order for this to work, the DOS command, GRAPHICS must be issued from the DOS system prompt prior to loading Lotus. The normal procedure, however, is to save the graph as a PIC file with the Graph Save command and then use the Lotus Print Graph program to produce the print-out.

The disadvantage to using the Lotus Print Graph program is that it is time consuming to create the graphs, save them, exit Lotus 1-2-3, call up the Lotus Print Graph program and print the graphs. The advantage is that the Lotus Print Graph program provides many options not available in either VP Planner or by producing a print screen print-out.

If you are re-entering Lotus, access the main Graph menu. (**/G**raph)

1. Select and save each file as a PIC file.
(**N**ame **U**se |highlight MKSHR 1980| <RET> **S**ave MS80P <RET>)

Note: Unlike the Name Create command, Save will create a separate disk file and requires the file to have a legitimate DOS file name. DOS allows up to eight characters in the root of the file name and Lotus will assign the PIC extension. Spaces are not legal characters for file names. The P in MS80P is used to indicate that this file is a pie chart. L and B will be use to represent line and bar graphs files respectively.

2. Select the remaining graphs and save them assigning the following names:

Graph Name	Save As
MKSHR 1984	MS84P
MKSHR 1987 PROJ	MS87PP
MKSHR 80-87PROJ	MS8087PL
SLS 80-87 PROJ1	SLS8087B
SLS 80-87 PROJ2	SLS8087L

3. Quit the Graph menu and exit Lotus.
(**Q**uit /**Q**uit **Y**es)

4. Enter the Lotus Print Graph program by selecting Print Graph from the Lotus Access menu.

5. Select Image-Select from the Print Graph main menu.
(**I**mage-**S**elect <RET>)

6. Mark each graph to be printed by moving through the list and pressing the space bar. After all of the graphs are marked, press <RET>.

Note: Depending upon your hardware configuration and whether or not the Print Graph program has been run on your system, you may have to specify the drive and/or directory that contains the graph (PIC) files and the drive and/or directory that contains the font (Lotus Print Graph) files.

If you are using a dual floppy drive system, the graph files will probably be in drive B and the font files will probably be in drive A. If you are using a hard drive system, your graph files should be in a subdirectory of the directory containing the Lotus program files, and the font files should be in the same directory as the Lotus program files. You may also have to specify the printer. These changes are made through the Hardware selection from the Settings menu. If you have problems, consult your instructor.

7. Position your paper in the printer and print the graphs.
(**A**lign **G**o)

It will take several minutes to print all of the graphs. After they are printed, you may exit the Print Graph program by selecting Exit from the main menu or you may want to experiment with the other options available.

Part F - One Step Beyond

There are many graph enhancement packages available such as Lotus Development Corporation's Free Lance, Software Publishing Corporation's Harvard Presentation Graphics, Computer Support Corporation's Picture Perfect that can do wonders to a standard PIC file. If you have access to one of these programs, use it to enhance the graphs created for the Bonger Bat Company.

EXERCISE 7

Amortization Schedule

Level Of Difficulty: [3]

Type of application: Accounting/Finance

Commands used:

    /**W**orksheet **E**rase
    /**W**orksheet **G**lobal **C**olumn Width
    /**W**orksheet **C**olumn **S**et
    /**W**orksheet **G**lobal **P**rotection
    /**W**orksheet **W**indows
    /**W**orksheet **G**lobal **R**ecalculation
    /**R**ange **U**nprotect
    /**R**ange **I**nput
    /**R**ange **F**ormat (Currency, Date, Fixed, Comma, Percent)
    /**C**opy
    /**P**rint

Functions Used:

    @SUM
    @DATE
    @YEAR
    @MONTH
    @DAY
    @IF
    @CHOOSE
    @ROUND
    @PMT

Techniques Used:

    Repeating label entries
    Copying multiple row form dividers
    Copying a row of formulas
    Positioning labels with spaces
    Complex date manipulation
    Nesting functions in formulas
    Splitting formula logic into separate cells

Special Keys:

    [F9] [F6]

PROBLEM

You have a new construction company. Although you have plenty of work and the long range outlook is good, you are having mild cash flow problems and are constantly borrowing money to meet your obligations. You need to know the payoff for the various loans and how much you are spending on interest.

ANALYSIS

Some of the loans are long term with payments every six months; others are short term with monthly payments. You want a worksheet that will show you the amount of the loan, who it is with, how much interest is being paid, and what the final payback factor will be if the loan goes to maturity. The worksheet must handle monthly, quarterly, semi-annual, and annual payments.

DESIGN

Following the basic design concept of separating the assumption area from the calculation area, this spreadsheet will have three basic sections. The assumption area will be located at the top and will accept the input values. The next area down will provide a summary of the calculations and contain most of the desired information. The calculation area will be directly below.

The following information is desired as a result of the calculations:

    Payment amount
    Total interest paid over the life of the loan
    Total principal paid back
    Total amount paid back (including interest)
    Payback factor (how many times the amount borrowed will be paid back)

The following data is required to provide the desired output:.

    Principal amount
    Annual interest rate
    Term of the loan in years
    Payment periods
    Date first payment is due

Occasionally, formulas can become so complex that it is helpful to split the logic into separate cells. This can not only simplify the formulas, but by doing so, can also save memory.

This particular amortization schedule allows 4 different payment periods. As long as the payment period contains either 1 or 12 months, the formula to calculate the next payment date is fairly simple. Since the @MONTH function recognizes only the values 1 through 12, a problem arises when adding the number of months in the payment period when the previous payment date exceeds 12. The formula that handles this problem must have access to the number of months in the payment period in four separate locations and in its condensed form (utilizing the formula in cell I1) is 120 characters long. The formula that calculates the number of months in the payment period (cell I1) is 22 characters long. Lotus 1-2-3, as well as most of the clones, will allow up to 240 characters to be entered into a single cell as either a label or a formula. Writing the formula to determine the number of months in the payment period 4 times would require 88 characters, while referencing cell I1 4 times requires only 16. Thus, for every cell that calculates the payment date in the calculation area, we save 72 characters. A five-year loan with monthly payments requires 59 such calculations. A 30-year loan requires 359. Including 25,848 unnecessary characters in formulas in a large spreadsheet will not only substantially increase the calculation time, but the amount of memory wasted may cause you to run out of memory capacity before completing the spreadsheet.

DEVELOPMENT

Part A - Create Screen

1. Starting with a clear worksheet, set the global column width to 12.
(**/W**orksheet **G**lobal **C**olumn-Width **12** <RET>)

2. Move cursor to the following columns and set the widths shown.
(**/W**orksheet **C**olumn **S**et **16** <RET>)

Column	Width
A	17
C	19

3. Create the screen shown in FIGURES 7.1 and 7.2.
(Note: Precede all label entries with quote marks to right align, excluding form dividers.)

```
             A              B              C              D
1   LOAN AMORTIZATION SCHEDULE
2
3   ================================================================
4   PRINCIPAL AMOUNT:             TERM IN YEARS:
5
6    ANNUAL INTEREST:             PMTS MADE:
7                                   1=MONTHLY, 2=QUARTERLY
8                                   3=SEMI-ANNUALLY, 4=ANNUALLY
9       1ST PMT DATE:
10
11  ~~~~~~~~~~~~~~~~~~~~~~~~~~~~~~~~~~~~~~~~~~~~~~~~~~~~~~~~~~~~~~~~~
12
13  TOTAL # PMTS:                 TOTAL PRINCIPAL:
14
15   PMT AMOUNT:                  TOTAL INTEREST:
16
17   TOTAL PAID:                  PAYBACK FACTOR:
18
19  ----------------------------------------------------------------
20
21      PAYMENT #        DATE              AMOUNT   INTEREST  PRINCIPAL
```

FIGURE 7.1

```
             F              G              H          I          J          K
1
2
3    ====================
4
5
6
7
8
9
10
11   ~~~~~~~~~~~~~~~~~~~~
12
13
14
15
16
17
18
19   --------------------
20
21      ADD/PMT     BALANCE
```

FIGURE 7.2

Part B: Formula Entry:

1. To prevent the formulas to be written from producing error values, enter the following values in the corresponding cells:

Cell	Value
B4	2000
B6	.1575
D4	2
D6	1
A22	1
F22	0
F23	0

2. Enter the following formulas:

Cell	Formula
I1	@CHOOSE(D6,0,1,3,6,12)
B9	@DATE(87,10,15)
B13	+D4*@CHOOSE(D6,0,12,4,2,1)
D13	@SUM(E22..E90)
B15	

@ROUND(@PMT(B4,B6/@CHOOSE(D6,0,12,4,2,1),B13),2)

Cell	Formula
D15	@SUM(D22..D90)
B17	@SUM(C22..C90)
D17	+B17/D13 (Note: ERR is temporary)
B22	+B9
C22	+B15
D22	+B4*$B$6/@CHOOSE($D$6,0,12,4,2,1)
E22	+C22-D22
G22	+B4-E22-F22
A23	@IF(G22>0,A22+1,0)
B23	

@DATE(@YEAR(B22)+@IF(@MONTH(B22)+$I$1>12,1,0),@IF(@MONTH
(B22)+$I$1>12,(@MONTH(B22)+$I$1)-12,@MONTH(B22)+$I$1),
@DAY(B22))

C23
@IF(G22>0.005,@IF(G22>1.1*$B$15,$B$15,G22+D23),0)

Cell	Formula
D23	+G22*$B$6/@CHOOSE($D$6,0,12,4,2,1)
E23	+C23-D23
G23	+G22-E23-F23

3. Set the following range formats:

Cell or Range	Format
B4	Currency, 2 decimals
B6	Percent, 2 decimals
B9	Date 1 (dd-mmm-yy)
B15..B17	Currency, 2 decimals
D13..D15	Currency, 2 decimals
D17	Fixed, 2 decimals
B22..B90	Date 1 (dd-mmm-yy)
C22..F90	, (Comma), 2 decimals
G22..G90	Currency, 2 decimals

4. Copy cell range A23..G23 to A24..A90.
(/**C**opy {from} **A23..G23** <RET> {to} **A24..A90** <RET>)

5. Turn the worksheet protection on.
(/**W**orksheet **G**lobal **P**rotection **E**nable)

6. Unprotect cells B4, B6, B9, D4, and D6.
(/**R**ange **U**nprotect **B4..B4** <RET>)

7. To automate cursor movement, issue the Range Input command, highlighting cells A1..D10 as the input range.
(/**R**ange **I**nput **A1..D10** <RET>)

Note: The Range Input command will allow the cursor to move to only the cells that have been unprotected with the Range Unprotect command.

8. Using [Right] instead of <RET>, enter several values for the assumptions and observe the results.

9. To cancel the Range Input command, press [**Esc**].

10. Notice that there is a delay while the spreadsheet recalculates every time there is an entry made. To speed up the data entry process on large spreadsheets, turn the recalculation mode to manual.
(/**W**orksheet **G**lobal **R**ecalculation **M**anual)

11. Make an entry and notice the CALC indicator in the lower right corner of the screen.

12. Complete the entries and press [F9] to recalculate the spreadsheet. Notice that the CALC indicator goes off.

13. Move the cursor to A12 and split the screen horizontally.
(/**W**orksheet **W**indows **H**orizontal)

14. Move the cursor to the lower window.
([**F6**])

15. Scroll the screen up so that line 21 is below the ~ divider allowing you to view a portion of the calculation area.

16. Move the cursor back to the upper screen. ([**F6**])

17. Change PMTS MADE: to 4, then press [F9] and notice how the PAYMENT DATE changes.

18. Using condensed print, print an amortization schedule for each of the following set of values: (Stop the print range when the balance = 0. Remember to set the right margin wide enough to include column G.)

	PRINCIPAL	INTEREST	1ST PMT DATE	TERM	PERIOD
1	$2,000	18%	Jul 1, 1986	1.5 yrs	Monthly
2	5,000	10%	Jan 15, 1988	3 yrs	Annually
3	75,000	12%	Nov 9 1984	7 yrs	Semi Annual
4	25,000	9.75%	Feb 17, 1988	5 yrs	Quarterly

19. Unprotect cells F22..F90.
(/**R**ange **U**nprotect **F22..F90** <RET>)

20. Reprint number 4, making a 1,000 dollar additional payment (ADD/PMT) every May.

21. Save this file as EX7.
(/**F**ile **S**ave **EX7** <RET>)

Part C - One Step Beyond

There are several other formulas other than column B that use a decision process repetitively. Find and re-write these formulas using the split-cell formula technique. Assign range names to the referenced cells to further simplify the writing and understanding of these formulas.

EXERCISE 8

Customer Database

Level Of Difficulty: [3]

Type of Application: Marketing

Commands Used:

    /Worksheet Insert Column
    /Worksheet Global Format
    /Range Format
    /Range Name (Create, Delete)
    /Range Erase
    /Data Query (Find, Extract)
    /Data Fill
    /Data Sort
    /Print Printer Options (Set-up, Margins)
    /Copy
    /Move

Functions Used:

    @SUM

Techniques Used:

    Sorting a database
    Using Data Fill to number records to return the
    database to the original order
    Using Data Query Find and Extract
    Utilizing a moving Data Query Output range to create
    reports

Special Keys:

    [F7] [F3] [F5]

Special Requirements:

Wide carriage printer is recommended but not necessary for
the first three reports.

Control codes listed are for EPSON emulation. For use with
alternate printer, substitute appropriate code for condensed
print.

PROBLEM

You work in the marketing department of a large wholesale company that sells stereos, appliances, and industrial electrical components to retail stores and supply houses. In addition, there is a small retail division that sells stereos to consumers. One of your responsibilities is to provide the marketing director with quarterly reports on product sales, sales staff performance, and customer purchase volumes.

ANALYSIS

You are required to produce the following quarterly reports:

1. An alphabetical listing of all customers.

2. An alphabetical listing of customers sorted by customer type.

3. A list of customer's year-to-date purchase amounts sorted by customer type and listed in descending order.

4. A list of customers sorted by customer type and grouped by the type products they purchase.

5. Year-to-date sales totals for each salesperson.

6. A list of all customers who purchased $50,000 or more of merchandise.

The last three reports must fit on 8-1/2 x 11 inch paper.

DESIGN

Maintaining the data and providing the reports can be accomplished by using the database capabilities provided by either VP-Planner or Lotus 1-2-3. This will require two separate spreadsheet areas. First, you will need a database area designed to contain all of the necessary data. Second, you will need a query/report area in which to extract data from the database and to create the reports. The database should contain the following fields:

Customer	Phone
Address	Contact
City	Customer Type
State	Salesman
Zip Code	Product Type
	Year-To-Date Purchases

The Query/Report area will contain the same field structure as the database and will be located immediately to the right. The query criterion range will be at the top of this area followed by the report text and a movable Data Query Output range. This will give flexibility to the reporting capabilities without having to create a complicated macro program.

DEVELOPMENT

<u>Part A - Set up a Database</u>

1. Starting with a clear worksheet, set the following column widths:

Column	Width
A	24
B	24
C	14
D	4
E	11
F	16
G	20
H	11
I	10
J	10
K	11
M	24
N	24
O	14
P	4
Q	11
R	16
S	20
T	11
U	10
V	10
W	11

2. Make the following cell entries:

Cell	Content
A1	Acme Wholesale
A2	Customer List
B2	Last Updated:
C2	{today's date}

3. Use repeating label prefix (\), then Copy command to produce a dashed from cell A3 to cell K3.
(\- <RET>)
(/Copy {from} **A3..A3** {to} **B3..K3** <RET>)

4. Enter the following field names in their corresponding columns in row 4:

Column	Field Name
A	Customer
B	Address
C	City
D	St
E	Zipcode
F	Phone
G	Contact
H	Cust.Type
I	Slsperson
J	Product
K	$ YTD

5. Starting on line 5, enter the following customer data in the proper columns:

Row 5:   Boyd Corporation   West 2285 Pines Rd.
        Vancouver   WA   98665   (206) 244-5536
        John Johnson Wholesale JR APPL   1455989

Row 6:   Anderson Stereo   436 W. Main
        Vancouver   WA   98665   (206) 244-3465
        Sally Masters Wholesale JR STR   325466

Row 7:   Mike Watson   18566 Colfax Rd. #45
        Spokane   WA   99218   (509) 466-5762
                   Retail   CS STR   1245

Row 8:   Allen Healy   S. 14367 198th
        Spokane   WA   99324   (509) 438-5438
                   Retail   CS STR   1745

Row 9:   Michaelson Electric   243 Main St.
        Chewelah   WA   99109   (509) 938-3445
        Allen Johnson Wholesale MS ELE   56967

Row 10: Mark Jones   E. 2334 23rd
        Spokane   WA   99203   (509) 546-6543
                   Retail   CS APPL   3576

Row 11: Appliance World   W. 3456 Marquette
        Spokane   WA   99207   (509) 437-7865
        Annie Kroft   Wholesale FJ APPL   65876

Row 12: Mike Thompson   W. 3546 54th
        Spokane   WA   99204   (509) 354-4655
                   Retail   CS STR   1507

Row 13: Acme Electric   West 325 Maple Ave.
        Boise   ID   78435   (208) 435-5469
        Dave Mason   Wholesale MS ELE   675899

```
Row 14:  K & D Supply                      W. 5436 Waiversly
         Boise           ID    78435       (208) 324-5697
         Tom Weaton      Wholesale    MS   ELE       567456

Row 15:  Sally Smith                       45334 W. 29th
         Spokane         WA    99204       (509) 324-2547
                         Retail       CS   STR          895

Row 16:  Boyd's Appliance                  W. 4329 29th
         Kennewick       WA    98320       (509) 567-7865
         John Allen      Wholesale    FJ   APPL      947786

Row 17:  The Stereo Shop                   4533 Elm St.
         Coeur d'Alene   ID    78453       (208) 537-6756
         Marsha Dryer    Wholesale    MS   STR        35466

Row 18:  White's Electric                  76544 45th SE
         Bellevue        WA    98006       (206) 456-6756
         John White      Wholesale    JR   ELE       546767

Row 19:  S & S Electrical Supply           143 North Ave.
         Kalispell       MT    86555       (403) 675-8765
         Chuck Sampson   Wholesale    AN   ELE       995675

Row 20:  Clonker Associates                17715 Rimrock
         Valley          ID    78956       (208) 435-6765
         Mike Anderson   Wholesale    MS   STR       234556

Row 21:  Tom Brodrick                      5436 Government Way
         Coeur d'Alene   ID    78453       (208) 773-4325
                         Retail       CS   STR          575

Row 22:  Johnson Engineering               65745 23rd SE
         Seattle         WA    98198       (206) 546-7858
         Mark Johnson    Wholesale    JR   ELE      1546771

Row 23:  B & B Stereo                      3453 W. 5th
         Spokane         WA    99204       (509) 345-4335
         Stan Bailey     Wholesale    MS   STR       786546

Row 24:  Anderson Stereo                   S. 14356 Oak
         Portland        OR    87678       (503) 453-8764
         Larry Leaves    Wholesale    JR   STR       458998
```

6. Format column K to display commas with no decimals.
(/Range Format , (Comma) **0** <RET> **K5..K24** <RET>)

Part B - Sorting Data

Both Lotus 1-2-3 and VP-Planner will allow either single or double fields sorts. An example of a single field sort would be a list of people in ascending or descending order according to age. An example of a double field sort would be a telephone book where the names are listed alphabetically by both last and first names. Using the last name as the first sort field or primary key causes the last names to appear in alphabetical order. The second field, the first name, is sorted only when there is more than one person with the same last name. By using two sort keys, we are able to cause Mary Clark to be listed before Tom Clark even if Tom Clark appeared before Mary Clark in the original database.

Before we sort the database, it is a good idea to set up some method to return the database to the original order. The easiest way to do this is to use the Data Fill command to number the records before they are sorted.

1. Move the cursor to cell A1 and insert a blank column.
(/**W**orksheet **I**nsert **C**olumn **A1..A1** <RET>)

2. Number the records.
(/**D**ata **F**ill **A5..A24** <RET> {Start} 1 <RET> {Step} 1 <RET> {Stop} <RET>)

Note: In this instance, it is not necessary to specify a "Stop" value as the Data Fill command will only fill the range specified (A5..A24) and the default "Stop" value is greater than the largest number that will be produced by the command within the specified range.

3. Sort in ascending order on the Customer field.
(/**D**ata **S**ort **D**ata-Range **A5..L24** <RET> **P**rimary-Key B5 <RET> A <RET> Go)

4. Print the alpha sort omitting the record numbers.
(/**P**rint **P**rinter **R**ange **B1..L24** <RET> **O**ptions **S**etup \015 <RET> **M**argins **R**ight 132 <RET> **Q**uit **A**lign **G**o **P**age **Q**uit)

Note: If you do not have a wide carriage printer, reduce the width of columns F & G as follows:

Spreadsheet	Do This
VP-Planner	Set width to 0
Lotus 1-2-3 1A	Set width to 1
Lotus 1-2-3 2.0+	Hide columns F & G

(/**W**orksheet **C**olumn **H**ide **F1** <RET>)

5. Sort with Cust.Type as the primary key in descending order and Customer as the Secondary Key in ascending order. (/**Data Sort Data-Range A5..L24** <RET> **Primary-Key I5** <RET> **D** <RET> **Secondary-Key B5** <RET> **A** <RET> Go)

6. Print the customer type/alpha sort omitting the record numbers (follow Step 4).

7. Sort with Cust.Type as the Primary Key in descending order and $ YTD as the Secondary Key in ascending order. (/**Data Sort Data-Range A5..L24** <RET> **Primary-Key I5** <RET> **D** <RET> **Secondary-Key L5** <RET> **A** <RET> **G**o)

8. Print customer purchases year-to-date (follow Step 4).

Part C - Performing Queries

Using the Data Sort command provides certain reporting capabilities that may not be flexible enough to create a particular report without disturbing the database. The Data Query commands allow records to be located or extracted from the database without altering the database.

The Data Query Find command requires the definition of a criterion range in which the records being sought are described. The Data Query Extract command requires both a criterion range which describes the data to be extracted and an output range where the data being extracted can be written. It is convenient to assign range names to these areas to facilitate changes from one query to another.

A. Data Query Find

1. To assure that the field names appear in the criterion range exactly as they appear in the database range, copy the field names in the database range (cells B4..L4) to cells N1..X1. (/**Copy** {from} **B4..L4** <RET> {to} **N1** <RET>)

2. Assign the range name "DB" to the database. (/**Range Name Create** <u>DB</u> <RET> **A4..L24** <RET>)

3. Assign the range name "CRIT" to cells N1..X2. (/**Range Name Create** <u>CRIT</u> <RET> **N1..X2** <RET>)

4. To find all of JR's customers, move cursor to cell V2 and enter JR.

5. Set up Data Query Ranges and Find records. (/**Data Query Input** <u>DB</u> <RET> **Criterion** <u>CRIT</u> <RET> **F**ind)

Each time the down arrow key is pressed, the cursor will jump to the next record, matching the criterion until it finds the last record in the database that matches. Pressing the up arrow key will reverse the process.

> 6. Return to the READY mode.
>   (<RET> **Q**uit)

7. The function key, F7, will re-execute the previously executed Data Query command. Change the salesperson's initials in cell V2 to CS and press the function key F7. Use the down arrow [DOWN] to view the matching records.

B. Data Query Extract

In order to use the Data Query Extract command, it is necessary to create an output range. The field names in the output range must exactly match the field names in the database and criterion ranges. Therefore it is best to copy either the database or the criterion field names to the output range.

> 1. Copy the field names from the database to the output range.
>   (/**C**opy {from} **B4..L4** <RET> {to} **N11** <RET>)

> 2. Assign the range name OP to cells N11..X11.
>   (/**R**ange **N**ame **C**reate <u>OP</u> <RET> **N11..X11** <RET>)

> 3. Set up Data Query Extract Output range and Extract data .
>   (/**D**ata **Q**uery **O**utput <u>OP</u> <RET> **E**xtract **Q**uit)

All of the records containing CS as the salesperson should appear below the output range field names

Part D - Creating Reports with Data Query

By moving the Data Query Output range, it is possible to create reports that contain data from multiple queries and text written for the report.

A. Customer/Product/Volume Report

> 1. Erase cells N12..X17.
>   (/**R**ange **E**rase **N12..X17** <RET>)

2. Enter the following report heading in the corresponding cells:

Cell	Text
P4	Acme Wholesale Company
P5	Customer/Product/Volume Report
P6	{todays date}
N10	Report period: January 1, 198A - September 1, 198A
N14	Product Classification: Electrical

3. Use the F2 function key (edit) to insert spaces to center "Acme Wholesale Company" and the date in relation to "Customer/Product/Volume Report".

4. Sort the database with Cust.Type as the Primary Key and $ YTD as the Secondary Key. Specify descending order for both keys. (Refer to Part B if necessary.)

5. Erase all entries in second row of the criterion range. (/Range Erase **N2..X2** <RET>)

6. Move the Data Query Output range (cells N11..X11) to cells N15..X15.
(/Move {from} **OP** <RET> {to} **N15** <RET>)

7. Enter ELE in the Products (W2) column of the criterion range. Move cursor to the OP range and perform query.
([**F5**][**F3**] |highlight **OP**| <RET> [**F7**])

8. Move the Data Query Output range to cell N25.
(/Move {from} **OP** <RET> {to} **N25** <RET>)

9. Change the product in the criterion range to APPL (appliances). Move cursor to the OP range and perform query.
([**F5**][**F3**] |highlight **OP**| <RET> [**F7**])

10. Make the following cell entries:

Cell	Content
N24	Product classification: Appliances

11. Move the Data Query Output range to cell N33.
(/Move {from} **OP** <RET> {to} **N33** <RET>)

12. Change the product in the criterion range to STR (Stereos). Move cursor to the OP range and perform query.
([**F5**][**F3**] |highlight **OP**| <RET> [**F7**])

13. Make the following cell entries:

Cell	Content
N32	Product classification: Stereos

14. Change the following column widths:

Column	Width
O	0
P	16
Q	4
R	0
S	0
T	0
U	0
W	0
X	12

Note: With Lotus 1-2-3 Release 1A, use 1 instead of zero.
With Lotus 1-2-3 Release 2.0 and 2.01, use Worksheet Column
Hide to hide the columns listed for zero widths. With VP-
Planner, moving the cursor into a cell set to a width of
zero causes the cursor to disappear. Continue to press the
left or right arrow until the cursor re-appears.

15. Move OP range to row 12.
(/Move {from} **OP** {to} **N12** <RET>)

16. Cancel the condensed print code by specifying \018 as
the Set-Up code from the Print Printer Options menu. Print
the report using P4..X45 as the print range.
(/**P**rint **P**rinter **O**ptions **S**et-Up **\018** <RET> **Q**uit **R**ange **N4..X45**
<RET> **A**lign **G**o **Q**uit)

B. Sales Department Performance Report

Lotus 1-2-3 and VP-Planner both provide a way to control the
fields listed by a Data Query Extract operation other than
by setting the column width to zero or hiding the column.
The Data Query Extract command will extract only the fields
contained in the output range. By copying only the desired
fields to the output range, the remaining fields in the
database will be ignored by the extract operation.

   1. Erase cells N2..X60.
   (/**R**ange **E**rase **N2..X60** <RET>)

   2. Set the following column widths:
   (/**W**orksheet **C**olumn **S**et {width} <RET>)

   Note: If you are using Lotus 1-2-3 Release 2, first
   unhide the columns hidden in step 12.

Column	Width
O	14
P	6
Q	10
R	16

```
S                        20
T                        11
U                        10
W                        10
X                        12
```

3. Enter the following report heading in the corresponding cells:

Cell	Text
V2	JR
O4	Acme Wholesale Company
O5	Sales Department Performance Report
O6	{today's date}
N10	Report period: January 1, 1986 - September 1, 1986
N14	Salesperson: JR

4. Use the F2 function key to edit cells O4 and O6 to insert enough additional spaces to center the company name and date with the report title.

5. Format cells R4..R60 to , (Comma) with 0 decimal places.
(**/R**ange **F**ormat **,** (Comma) **0** <RET> **R4..R60** <RET>)

6. Copy the following field names from the criterion range (N1..X1) to the designated cells.
(**/C**opy {from} [From Cell] <RET> {to} [To Cell] <RET>)

Field Name	From Cell	To Cell
Customer	N1	N15
City	P1	O15
St	Q1	P15
Slsperson	V1	Q15
$ YTD	X1	R15

7. Re-assign range name OP to cells N15..R15.
(**/R**ange **N**ame **D**elete OP <RET>)
(**/R**ange **N**ame **C**reate OP <RET> **N15..R15** <RET> Quit)

8. Re-set Data Query Output range.
(**/D**ata **Q**uery **O**utput OP <RET>)

9. Move the output range from row 12 to row 15.
(**/M**ove {from} OP <RET> {to} **N15** <RET>)

10. Move cursor to the OP range and perform query.
([**F5**][**F3**] |highlight **OP**| <RET> [**F7**])

11. Make the following cell entries:

Cell	Content
N14	Salesperson: JR
P22	Total Sales:
R22	@SUM(R16..R20)

12. Change the salesperson in cell V2 to AN.
(**AN** <RET>)

13 Move the output range to cells N25..R25.
(/Move {from} **OP** {to} **N25** <RET>)

14. Move cursor to the OP range and perform query.
([**F5**][**F3**] |highlight **OP**| <RET> [**F7**])

15. Make the following cell entries:

Cell	Content
N24	Salesperson: AN
P28	Total Sales:
R28	+R26

16. Change the salesperson in cell V2 to MS.
(**MS** <RET>)

17. Move the output range to cells N31..R31.
(/Move {from} **OP** {to} **N31** <RET>)

18.Move cursor to the OP range and perform query.
([**F5**][**F3**] |highlight **OP**| <RET> [**F7**])

19. Make the following cell entries:

Cell	Content
N30	Salesperson: MS
P39	Total Sales:
R39	@SUM(R32..R37)

20. Change the salesperson in cell V2 to FJ.
(**FJ** <RET>)

21. Move the output range to cells N43..R43.
(/Move {from} **OP** {to} **N43** <RET>)

22. Move cursor to the OP range and perform query.
([**F5**][**F3**] |highlight **OP**| <RET> [**F7**])

23. Make the following cell entries:

Cell	Content
N42	Salesperson: FJ
P47	Total Sales:
R47	@SUM(R44..R45)

24. Change the salesperson in cell V2 to CS.
(**CS** <RET>)

25. Move the output range to cells N51..R51.
(/Move {from} **OP** {to} **N51** <RET>)

26. Move cursor to the OP range and perform query.
([**F5**][**F3**] |highlight **OP**| <RET> [**F7**])

27. Make the following cell entries:

Cell	Content
N50	Salesperson: CS
P59	Total Sales:
R59	@SUM(R52..R57)

28. Using /Range Format Currency 0, format the total sales amounts to currency with 0 decimal places.

29. Move the output range to cells N12..R12.
(/Move {from} **OP** {to} **N12** <RET>)

30. Print report. (refer to Part B, step 4 if necessary)

C. Preferred Customer List

The previous reports were created by specifying a single text criterion. The next report will use the Data Query command's capability to utilize multiple fields and formulas in the Query Criterion range.

1. Erase cells N13..R59.
(/Range Erase **N13..R59** <RET>)

2. Erase cell V2.
(/Range Erase **V2** <RET>)

3. Change cell O5 to read: "Preferred Customer List"
Note: Do not include the quote marks (").

4. Enter the following formula in cell X2: **+L5>10000**

5. Perform query.
([**F7**])

6. Position paper in printer and print report.
(/**P**rint **P**rinter **R**ange **N4..R23** <RET> **A**lign **G**o)

The Data Query command works by applying a filter specified
by the criterion range to the records in the Data Query
Input range and allowing only records matching the field
contents specified in the Data Query Criterion range to
filter through to the output range. In the previous query,
only records containing values greater than 100000 in the $
YTD field passed through the filter to the output range.

The next report will display all customers in the state of
Washington that purchased over $100,000 worth of products.

7. Enter "WA" in cell Q2.
Note: Do not include the quote marks.

8. Perform query.
([**F7**])

9. Print report.

10. Return the database to its original order by sorting it
in ascending order with A5 specified as the primary key.
(/**D**ata **S**ort {Range} **A5..L24** <RET> **P**rimary-Key **A5** <RET> **G**o)

11. Move cursor to cell A1 and delete column A.
(/**W**orksheet **D**elete **C**olumn **A1..A1** <RET>)

12. Save file as EX8.
(/**F**ile **S**ave **EX8** <RET>)

Part E - One Step Beyond

Both Lotus 1-2-3 and VP-Planner support the MS-DOS wildcard
characters asterisk (*) and question mark (?) for Data Query
Criterion specifications when used with label
entries. By entering the zip codes as labels, it is
possible to enter 9* in the Zipcode field of the criterion
range to extract all of the records that have zip codes
starting with a 9. Entering S* in the Customer field will
produce all customers whose names start with an S. The
asterisk (*) will substitute for any character and any
number of characters. The question mark substitutes on a
one-to-one basis. To obtain all of the records with zip
codes starting with a 9 using the question mark as the wild
card character, it is necessary to enter 9???? in the
Zipcode field of the Data Query Criterion range.

Experiment with wildcards and formulas to see the many
different possible ways to query a Lotus 1-2-3 or VP-Planner
database.

CONTENTS

Page

************* C R E A T I N G   A   D A T A B A S E *************

EXERCISE 1

Creating a Client List

Commands used:	CREATE
	LIST
Level of difficulty:	[1]
Type of application:	[Marketing]
Purpose:	To introduce the student to the importance of planning and structuring a database

PROBLEM:

You have just been hired by the private detective agency
Remington Iron to computerize their client file. Presently the
firm is keeping the name and address of agency clients on matchbook covers stored in a shoe box (SEE FIGURE 1). The agency
owner, Rusty Iron, likes to contact previous clients to check on
the possibility of additional business. He would like to be able
to locate their addresses without digging through an entire shoe
box. Your job is to set up a database that allows the owner to
find addresses quickly and easily.

Bill Johnson
South 2000 15th
Bellevue, WA 89000

FIGURE 1.1

ANALYSIS:

Upon examining several matchbook covers, a pattern begins to
emerge. First, you notice that each cover has both a first and
last name, street address, city, state, and zip code. After
questioning Mr. Iron further, you discover that he wants to
locate client information based on all of these categories.
Thus, each category or "field" must be established as unique in
your database. For example, if you wish to search for the last
name "Johnson" and have entered "Bill Johnson" in the field, the
computer will be unable to locate it. Last name must be a
separate field from first name.

Second, with your knowledge of dBase III Plus you realize that, beyond planning for field names, you must also specify the type of field needed for storing information. Since the nature of this database precludes the need for computations, dates, or extended text, you will use only the character field type.

The third fact uncovered in your investigation is the width required for each field. For instance, you noticed that all the last names are less than 20 characters in width. When you specify the field width for last name you can set it at 20.

It should be obvious, at this point, that planning is essential to the successful creation of a database. The structure of a computerized database is quite rigid and although dBase III Plus does allow for alterations at a later date, much time and pain can be saved by a little forethought during creation.

DEVELOPMENT:

Part A

1. CREATE a file named AGENCY. (dBase III Plus file names must be 8 characters or less with no spaces.)

2. Enter the field names, types, and widths in FIGURE 2.

Field Name	Type	Width	Dec
lname	character	20	
fname	character	15	
address	character	40	
city	character	20	
state	character	2	
zip	character	9	

FIGURE 1.2

3. Save the database structure you just created and go to the dot prompt. To get a hard copy of your database structure, type:

LIST STRUCTURE TO PRINT <RET>

Part B

1.   CREATE a database file called DETECTOR. (dBase III Plus file names must be 8 characters or less with no spaces.)

2.   Enter the database structure list in FIGURE 1.3. Assume that the agency owner has changed his mind and would now like to have a contact date for each client.

Field Name	Type	Width	Dec
lastname	character	20	
firstname	character	15	
street	character	40	
city	character	20	
state	character	2	
zip	character	9	
date	date	8	

FIGURE 1.3

3.   Save the database structure you just created and go to the dot prompt. To get a hard copy of your database structure, type:

LIST STRUCTURE TO PRINT   <RET>

Part C

1.   CREATE a database file called CLIENT. (dBase III Plus file names must be 8 characters or less with no spaces.)

2.   Enter the database structure listed in FIGURE 1.4. Assume the owner has decided he wants to record both the date a client is first contacted and the name of his company.

Field Name	Type	Width	Dec
lastname	character	20	
firstname	character	15	
company	character	25	
street	character	40	
city	character	20	
state	character	2	
zip	character	9	
date	date	8	

FIGURE 1.4

3. Save the database structure you just created and go to the
dot prompt. To get a hard copy of your database structure, type:

LIST STRUCTURE TO PRINT <RET>

EXERCISE 2

Check Register

Commands used:	CREATE APPEND LIST USE SUM
Level of difficulty:	[2]
Type of application:	[Accounting]
Purpose:	This exercise requires the student to design his/her own database structure including field names, types, and widths. Records must then be entered using the APPEND command.

PROBLEM:

Every business is faced with the task of disbursing funds.
Often, those transactions are recorded in a check register. When
the register is a paper ledger, locating a particular check can
be difficult. It is also a hardship to reconcile a manual
system, while a database check register is relatively quick and
easy to use.

Your task is to use the facts given in the analysis section of
this case to construct a check register for the "Day Old Yogurt
Shop." This company is a one person operation which opened its
doors at the beginning of the year.

ANALYSIS:

To complete this exercise, you will need to use all of the field
types available in dBase III Plus. You must decide on a name and
width for each field. The information to be entered in the

database is listed in FIGURE 2.1. Examine it carefully before
establishing the database structure. (Remember, if a field is to
store numbers for calculation, it should be set up as a Numeric
type.)

CH	PAID TO	AMOUNT	DATE	REMARKS [Memo Field]
101	Day Old Dairy	$451.00	02/03/87	To pay January's bill.
102	Uncle Morris	$200.00	02/09/87	To pay on family note.
103	Mr. Turnbol	$500.00	02/28/87	Rent for March.
104	Edison Power	$ 43.00	03/02/87	February's utility bill.
105	Slick Eddie	$900.00	03/04/87	Attorney fees.
106	Pete Zundle	$ 50.00	03/07/87	Cleaning services.

FIGURE 2.1

DEVELOPMENT:

Part A

1.   CREATE a structure for the check register database.
(Remember that your database name must be 8 characters or less.)

2.   Save the structure and return to the dot prompt.

3.   Enter the 6 records listed in FIGURE 2.1 by first typing:

APPEND <RET>

(If you happen to press the <RET> key before typing anything in
the first field of a new record, dBase III Plus will jump out of
the Entry Mode back to the dot prompt. Just type APPEND to
return to the place you left off. To enter data in the memo
field, use the <CTRL><PgDn> keys to turn on the memo field and
the <CTRL><PgUp> keys to turn it off.)

4.   Use the <CTRL><END> keys to save the records when you are
done.

5.   Examine your database by typing:

LIST <RET>

(This will cause the records in your database to be displayed
horizontally.)

6.   Now print a copy of your database by typing:

LIST TO PRINT <RET>

7. Print a copy of your database structure by typing:

             LIST STRUCTURE TO PRINT   <RET>

Part B

1. CREATE the structure for the check register database with a
different file name than used in Part A. In addition to the
fields needed to capture the data in FIGURE 1.3 on page 4, add a
logical field. This field can be used to mark each record with a
"T" or "F" as a verification procedure during check
reconciliation.

2. Enter the records in FIGURE 2.1 on page 6 with no entry for
the logical field.

3. Print out a list of the database records and structure.

Part C

1. USE the database created in Part B. The USE command can be
entered at the dot prompt, followed by a space and the name of
the database, to cause that database to be available for
commands. (e.g. USE XXXXXXX <RET>)

2. APPEND the records in FIGURE 2.2.

CH	PAID TO	AMOUNT	DATE	REMARKS
107	Modern Office	$500.00	03/08/87	To pay for office equip.
108	Superior Ads	$630.00	03/22/87	To pay for advertisement.
109	Mr. Turnbol	$500.00	03/28/87	To pay April rent.

                       FIGURE 2.2

3. Print a list of all the records.

4. At the dot prompt type:

             SUM(AMOUNT)   <RET>

The SUM command will cause dBase III Plus to add all of the
numbers in the AMOUNT field and display the answer.

5. To print out the SUM of the AMOUNT field, press the <CTRL>
and <P> key together. (This turns on a port to the printer so
that everything you type will be both displayed on your monitor

and printed by your printer.) Now repeat step 4. After getting
the printout, turn off the port to the printer by again pressing
the <CTRL><P> keys.

************ E D I T I N G   A   D A T A B A S E ****************

EXERCISE 3

Parts List

Commands used:	CREATE
	EDIT
	BROWSE
	DELETE
	RECALL
	PACK
	LIST

Level of difficulty:	[1]
Type of application:	[Operations Management]
Purpose:	This exercise uses the record level editing capabilities of dBase III Plus to make changes to a parts list.

PROBLEM:

You are the assistant operations manager for the Acme Robotics Company. The firm is presently experiencing both shortages and surpluses in their parts inventory for the production of their new robot model XY27. To improve the purchasing of parts for XY27, you have decided to create a parts list on dBase III Plus.

ANALYSIS:

After some research, you come up with the list of the parts necessary to assemble the robot. (See FIGURE 3.1.) Notice that besides the part number, description, and date of inventory for each part, there is also a quantity level. This quantity level can be used to notify the purchasing department when more parts are required.

PART NUMBER	DESCRIPTION	QUANTITY LEVEL	DATE
AB10:0112	right arm/hand	678	02/09/89
AB10:0101	left arm/hand	357	02/09/89
AB10:0109	head/sensors	567	02/09/89
AB10:0103	torso/cpo	490	02/09/89
AB10:0104	right leg/foot	30	02/09/89

FIGURE 3.1

DEVELOPMENT:

Part A

1. CREATE a database to store the facts listed in FIGURE 3.1.

2. Enter the records from FIGURE 3.1 in your database.

3. Use the EDIT command to correct an error in record 3. Change the PART NUMBER to AB10:0102 instead of the erroneous number AB10:0109.

4. Save the correction.

5. Now EDIT record 5. An inaccurate count placed the quantity of this part at 30. It is actually 359. Change the QUANTITY LEVEL to 359.

6. While still in EDIT, add the new record listed below:

AB10:0105   left leg/foot   400   02/09/89

7. Print a copy your database.

Part B

1. USE the database created in Part A.

2. Select the Browse Mode from Assist Menu or type BROWSE at the dot prompt.

3. Scan the database for record 4. Notice the entry in the DESCRIPTION field? It should read "torso/cpu" not "torso/cpo." Change it.

4. Now look for a record with 678 as a QUANTITY LEVEL. The shift manager has just informed you that 50 right arm/hand units have been used in production. Adjust the QUANTITY LEVEL to reflect the change.

5. Using BROWSE, find the record with the PART NUMBER AB10:0112. The number was recorded wrong and should be AB10:0100. Make the necessary adjustment.

6. Save the changes and print a copy of the database.

Part C

1.   USE the database created in Part A.

2.   DELETE record 2.

3.   LIST the database. Notice the asterisk in front of record 2.
This indicates that the record has been marked for deletion. The
record will not actually disappear until the PACK command is
issued.

4.   You can remove the asterisk with the RECALL command by
typing:

RECALL RECORD 2   <RET>

LIST the database again and note that the asterisk is now gone.

5.   DELETE all records with a QUANTITY LEVEL less than 400. (Do
not PACK.)

6.   DELETE the record where the field DESCRIPTION equals
"torso/cpu."   (Do not PACK.)

7.   Print a copy of your database.

EXERCISE 4

Personnel List

Commands used:
CREATE
USE
REPLACE
MODIFY STRUCTURE
LIST
DISPLAY
SET PRINT ON/OFF

Level of difficulty: [2]

Type of application: [Management]

Purpose: This exercise uses the file level editing capabilities of dBase III Plus to alter an entire database. The DISPLAY command is used to demonstrate dBase III Plus's ability to locate specific records.

PROBLEM:

As the new personnel manager for the Mansfield Insurance Company, you have discovered a problem. Mansfield is a regional company with offices in ten states. Your main office dispatches claim adjusters to investigate insurance claims. Because your firm is a full-line insurance company, claims can range from a simple auto accident to a large complex commercial disaster. Your claims adjusters are specialists, experts in one or more area of claims. For instance, one agent might have a vast background in airplane accidents, while another might be knowledgeable about in home-related incidents. Hence, the difficulty arises in quickly matching the most qualified adjuster with a specific claim. The present system is manual and requires a great deal of time and effort to arrive at a good match.

ANALYSIS:

You have decided to create a dBase III Plus field to help manage the assignment of claim cases. This database should contain the adjuster's name, area of expertise, and current assignment. (For purposes of this exercise, assume each adjuster has only one area of specialization.) A partial list of claim agents is shown in FIGURE 4.1.

NAME	AREA OF EXPERTISE	CURRENT ASSIGNMENT
John Thomas	Air Disasters	Seattle, WA
Don Phillips	Auto Accidents	Spokane, WA
Roy Stevens	Home Accidents	Spokane, WA
Ron Johnson	Medical Disability	Portland, OR
Sue Reed	Small Business Claims	Sacramento, CA
Ben Grimm	Industrial Accidents	Los Angeles, CA
Patty Flynn	Fire Damage	Boise, ID
Peter Parker	Flood Damage	Billings, MT
Ann Manny	Earthquakes	Crescent City, CA
Bill Kinner	Industrial Accidents	Boise, ID
Jim Hege	Home Accidents	Portland, OR

FIGURE 4.1

In your database planning, you realize that a particular record may need to be found by last name, area of expertise, or current assignment.

DEVELOPMENT:

Part A

1. Create a database and enter the records in FIGURE 4.1.

2. Return to the dot prompt.

3. Just as you finish, a claim comes in for a home accident. You can now test your system for finding a match between adjuster and claim. Use the DISPLAY command to locate all of the adjusters with Home Accident experience. To record your query and the answer, first turn on the printer port by typing:

      SET PRINT ON <RET>

Now issue the DISPLAY command. Substitute the field name you gave the Area of Expertise for the [<field name>] in the following command and be sure to observe the proper capitalization.

      DISPLAY ALL FOR [<field name>] = "Home Accidents" <RET>

When you complete the query, type:

      SET PRINT OFF <RET>

to turn the printer port off.

4. Another call comes in for an industrial accident claim in Boise, ID. Use the DISPLAY command to determine if an agent is presently in Boise. Turn on the printer port so that the query and answer are both printed out. (Hint: Use the .AND. operator to phrase the query for both the area of expertise and current assignment.)

PART B

1. After considering your new system, you suddenly realize that something is missing. Although you have one field to contain an adjuster's specialization, you have neglected to provide a field for a second area of expertise. Fortunately dBase III Plus provides for such oversights. You can modify the structure of your database with the MODIFY STRUCTURE command. If you QUIT dBase III Plus earlier, USE the same database now. Then type:

MODIFY STRUCTURE   <RET>

A screen similar to the one in FIGURE 4.2 will appear. At the top of the screen, you will see a menu with the various options available for modifing the structure of your database. The name of the database in USE is listed at the bottom. The upper right-hand corner of the screen contains the number of bytes remaining in the record. The center of the screen contains the field names, types, widths, and decimal places you have already defined. Study the menu of options. Notice that the <CTRL>/N key combination will insert a new field. To use this option, move the cursor to the field below where you want to insert a new field and press <CTRL>/N. A blank field entry will be inserted.

FIGURE 4.2

2.   FIGURE 4.3 contains the second area of expertise for each claims adjuster. To create a new field for this information:

>   Move the cursor to the last field.

>   Press the <CTRL>/N key together.
>   Enter a field name, type, and width to contain the information in Figure 4.3.

3.   To save the changes:

>   Press the <CTRL><END> keys together.

>   Press <RET> to confirm the changes.

4. Now use the EDIT command to add the information in FIGURE 4.3.

NAME	SECOND AREA OF EXPERTISE
John Thomas	Auto Accidents
Don Phillips	Small Business Claims
Roy Stevens	Air Disasters
Ron Johnson	
Sue Reed	Medical Disability
Ben Grimm	Fire Damage
Patty Flynn	
Peter Parker	Earthquakes
Ann Manny	Flood Damage
Bill Kinner	Home Accidents
Jim Hege	

FIGURE 4.3

5. Print a copy of the modified records in your database and the new structure.

PART C

1. Just as you finish, the general manager calls and requests the dates each of your claims adjusters were given their present assignments. It occurs to you that a date field in your database could handle future requests for assignment time quite nicely. Use the database modified in Part B, issue the MODIFY STRUCTURE and EDIT commands to add the information in FIGURE 4.4.

NAME	STARTING DATE OF CURRENT ASSIGNMENT
John Thomas	6/12/87
Don Phillips	6/23/87
Roy Stevens	6/10/87
Ron Johnson	7/01/87
Sue Reed	6/08/87
Ben Grimm	6/07/87
Patty Flynn	7/04/87
Peter Parker	6/28/87
Ann Manny	7/25/87
Bill Kinner	6/26/87
Jim Hege	7/01/87

FIGURE 4.4

2. It's the beginning of 1988 and all of your claims adjusters
have been requested to travel to the home office in Seattle,
Washington. Change the date of the current assignment and the
location of the current assignment of all adjusters to **1/05/88**
and **Seattle, WA.** Use the REPLACE command to accomplish both
tasks. Before you begin, SET PRINT ON to record your entries to
the printer.

        REPLACE ALL assignment WITH 'Seattle, WA' <RET>

        REPLACE ALL date WITH CTOD('01/05/88') <RET>

3. LIST your database and SET PRINT OFF before you QUIT dBase
III Plus.

****************** S O R T I N G ********************

EXERCISE 5

Sales Report

Commands used: CREATE
                           USE
                           SORT
                           INDEX
                           TOTAL
                           LIST

Level of difficulty: [2]

Type of application: [Marketing]

Purpose: This exercise demonstrates the
power of a database to sort records
to provide useful views of data.
The difference between SORT
and INDEX is highlighted.

PROBLEM:

As the assistant manager for a large west coast distributor of
stereo equipment, you often find yourself buried in paper work.
Perhaps your most time-consuming task is the preparation of the
monthly sales report. Each month you receive a list of sales
activity from the accounting department. FIGURE 5.1 lists a
small sample of the type of data you receive.

DEALER	REP	ITEM	QUANTITY	PRICE	AMOUNT
Sound Off	John Peterson	R101	12	200	2400
Stereo Store	Pete Phillips	C201	6	250	1500
Lafco Sound	John Peterson	T203	10	100	1000
Pacific Sound	Sue Miller	R101	20	200	4000
The Big Ear	Tony Gill	C201	40	250	10000
Joe's Stereo	Cindy Tally	R101	15	200	3000
Sound Off	John Peterson	C201	5	250	1250
Lafco Sound	John Peterson	R101	20	200	4000
Stereo Store	Pete Phillips	T203	14	100	1400
The Big Ear	Tony Gill	R101	30	200	6000
Sound-o-rama	Cindy Tally	R101	50	200	10000

FIGURE 5.1

Notice that the column labeled AMOUNT is the product of the
QUANTITY and PRICE columns (AMOUNT = QUANTITY X PRICE). The ITEM
column contains the identification code for the stereo products
carried by the distributor. For example, R101 stands for a Sound
Mate model 101 receiver. The REP category shows the sales
representative. Each rep is assigned a specific territory to
cover. The DEALER column indicates the stereo retailer who is
purchasing the item.

When the sales list arrives each month, you patiently reorganize
it based on the AMOUNT column. You arrange the records in a
descending order so that the highest sales are at the top of the
list. The general manager uses the rearranged list to evaluate
the performance of sales reps and dealers.

ANALYSIS:

Realizing that a computerized database is well suited for sorting
data, you have decided to use dBase III Plus to save time in
preparing the sales report.

Before you rush off to create this database, a bit of planning is
advisable. For instance, what information do you want to include
in your report? At present, you are merely reorganizing the
records by sales amount because of the time involved. But with
dBase III Plus's help, you can quickly organize the records by
such categories as sales rep or dealer. Grouping the records by
sales rep or dealer would enable the general manager to make a
more accurate evaluation of sales performance.

When creating the database, keep in mind the sorting
requirements. Be sure to create a unique field for each category
you wish to sort on. The fields you establish for sorting
purposes are referred to as **key fields**. They are, in effect, the
key to the order of a sorted database.

In this case, you want to produce three reports:

(1) a report sorted from highest to lowest sale;

(2) a report sorted by dealer; and

(3) a report sorted by sales representative.

DEVELOPMENT:

Part A

1. CREATE a database structure based on FIGURE 5.1 on page 19.

2. Enter the records in FIGURE 5.1 on page 19.

3. Print the database.

4. To complete the first report you must reorganize the records by sales AMOUNT, starting with highest sale descending to the lowest. To accomplish this, **SORT the database on the AMOUNT field in a descending order to a file called TEMP.** (HINT: Use the /D following the SORT command.)

5. USE the database TEMP.

6. Print TEMP. (The printout should look like FIGURE 5.2.)

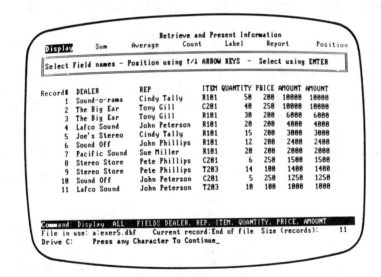

FIGURE 5.2

----

7. To create your second report ordered by dealer, you will need to SORT the records based on the DEALER field. SORT to a file called TEMP2. (By not specifying a "/D" the SORT command assumes you want to sort the database in an ascending order.)

8. USE and print TEMP2.

9. Create and print a third report sorted in an ascending order by REP.

Part B

Although sorting a file works fine to reorder records, it does have several drawbacks. First, because you are sorting the entire file, it is slow. Second, each time you sort, a new file is created. This can really eat up disk space when large databases are used. Finally, a sorted file does not allow for the most rapid location of information. (This topic will be covered in depth in the next exercise.)

The INDEX command is well named. Unlike the SORT command, INDEX does not create an entire database each time it is used. Instead, it creates a file with only the key field information and the record numbers associated with each key.

To create the three reports in Part A with the INDEX command, do the following:

1. USE your original database.

2. Use the INDEX command to sort the records in an ascending order based on AMOUNT field to a file named SALES.

3. Print the sorted records.

4. USE the original database.

5. INDEX in an ascending order on DEALER to a file named CUSTOMER.

6. Print the sorted records.

7. Use INDEX to create and print the third report (ascending).

Part C

The first two parts of this exercise taught you how to organize records. Although the sorting made it easier to spot the highest and lowest sale, it failed to show the **total** sales by item number, dealer, or sales representative. And this information is, after all, much more interesting in terms of how well your reps are performing or which dealer is responsible for the most sales. Fortunately, there is a dBase III Plus command which can perform these tasks. It's called TOTAL. The syntax for the command is listed below:

TOTAL ON <key field> TO <new file> FIELD <field name list>

This command will create subtotals for all like entries in a key field. (The key field must be indexed to use the TOTAL command.) When the command is given, dBase III Plus will go through the database looking at the entries in the specified key field. When the data in the key field changes, the program will create a new subtotal. The data in the subtotal becomes a record in the new database.

For example, in the sales report database created in Part A, you have six sales representatives. If you issue the following command, you will create a new database called reptotal with six records, each having a sales subtotal for that representative.

        TOTAL ON rep TO reptotal FIELDS rep,amount

Notice that the only fields listed at the end of the command are REP and AMOUNT. The other fields in the original database are not necessary for the report.

1. USE the original database created in Part A.

2. SET INDEX TO REPINDEX. (This index was created in Part B.)

3. Type:

        TOTAL ON rep TO reptotal FIELD rep,amount <RET>

4. USE reptotal.

5. LIST TO PRINT.

To create a report subtotaling each dealer's purchases, do the following:

1. USE the original database.

2. SET INDEX TO customer.

3. Type:

        TOTAL ON dealer TO dealtot FIELDS dealer,amount <RET>

4. USE dealtot.

5. LIST TO PRINT.

6. Create and print a report which subtotals sales by ITEM.

********************** S E A R C H I N G *************************

EXERCISE 6

Site Planning

Commands used: CREATE
                  USE
                  LIST
                  LOCATE
                  DISPLAY
                  CONTINUE
                  GO BOTTOM/TOP
                  INDEX
                  FIND

Level of difficulty: [2]

Type of application: [Marketing]

          Purpose: The power of a database program to sort
                      records is impressive but pales in
                      comparison to its ability to search
                      out a specific piece of information.
                      This exercise highlights the commands
                      available in dBase III Plus for locating
                      data.

PROBLEM:

You are planning to open your fourth Take & Bake Pizza shop. You
currently have three shops successfully operating in Spokane,
Washington. Your stores specialize in making a great tasting
pizza which people buy at your shop and then take home to bake.
Since the "take out" pizza market in Spokane has become over-
crowded and quite competitive, you are thinking of opening the
fourth store elsewhere.

FIGURE 6.1 is a list of cities you are considering for the new
store. The figure has four columns. The first column lists the
city name, while the next three columns contain selected
characteristics for each city. The second column shows a
competition rating factor based on a scale ranging from 1 to 10
(10 being the highest level and 1 the lowest.) This scale is
used to indicate the amount of "take out" pizza competition
present in the city. The third column lists the total population
for each city. The fourth column shows the annual food sales for
the city.

CITY	COMPETITION	POPULATION	ANNUAL FOOD SALES
TriCities	7	143900	$186346000
Seattle	10	491800	666242000
Tacoma	4	160300	190061000
Bellingham	3	46000	96941000
Everett	5	58000	101175000
Vancouver	2	43900	49865000
Yakima	1	49200	95186000

FIGURE 6.1

ANALYSIS:

You could narrow the number of possible sites for a new store based on any of the above city characteristics. For instance, if population is deemed the critical factor, you can quickly identify the cities with high populations. If competition becomes the key criterion, then the cities with low competition can be easily spotted in FIGURE 6.1. Food sales might be given the greatest importance and again the cities with high food sales could be quickly found. But what if you increased the number of cities or evaluation characteristics? What if you then wanted a list of cities with a population and annual food sales greater than a specific value and competition rating less than a given value? It would be quite difficult to find cities with these specific values from a large list of possibilities.

In an effort to avoid lengthy and time consuming searches, you have decided to create a computerized database. FIGURE 6.2 shows the structure for the database.

Field Name	Type	Width	Dec
CITY	Char/text	20	
COMPETE	Numeric	5	
POPULATION	Numeric	15	
FOOD_SALES	Numeric	15	

FIGURE 6.2

You can test this database by entering the small amount of data provided in FIGURE 6.1 and actually searching it for the best locations for the new store. It is often a good idea to design and test a database with a limited amount of data. In this way, changes can be made without vast data entry adjustments. This process is called **prototyping**.

DEVELOPMENT:

The factors of competition, population, and food sales will be
used to evaluate the attractiveness of various cities for a store
site. You can accomplish this in dBase III Plus by specifying
limits for each factor and then searching for the cities which
qualify. The LIST command will allow you to both set up limits
and display the results of a search.

Part A

After some consideration, you decide that a favorable location
must have a population of at least 70,000, a competition rating
of less than 6, and annual food sales of over $100,000,000.

1. CREATE a database from the suggestions in the Analysis
section on page 26.

2. Print a list of cities with a population greater than 70,000
by typing:

            LIST FOR POPULATION > 70000 TO PRINT <RET>

3. Print a list of cities with a competition rating of less
than 6.

4. Print a list of cities with annual food sales greater than
$100,000,000.

5. Now print a list of cities which match all three criteria by
typing:

LIST FOR POPULATION > 70000 .AND. FOOD_SALES > 100000000 .AND.
COMPETE < 6 TO PRINT <RET>

6. Upon reflection, you decide to change the search criteria.
The new limits are as follows:

            COMPETE   <= 7
            POPULATION   >   100000
            FOOD_SALES   >   80000000

Print a list of cities which meet these search parameters.

Part B

A close associate has suggested a particular population threshold for the new store. You can use the LOCATE command to find the cities that qualify.

1. Use the database created in Part A.

2. Type:

>   LOCATE FOR population > 150000 <RET>
>
>   DISPLAY TO PRINT <RET>

3. To see the next qualifying city in your database, type:

>   CONTINUE <RET>
>
>   DISPLAY TO PRINT <RET>

4. The GO TOP and GO BOTTOM commands position the record pointer at either the top or bottom of your database. Thus, when you issue the GO TOP command and then DISPLAY the current record, you will see the first record in your database.

Print the first and last record in your database with the aid of the GO command.

5. Use the LOCATE and DISPLAY commands to print the records with a competition rating of 1 or 2.

Part C

With the few records currently in your database, searching is a quick process. However, as your database grows in size, the speed in locating a record will decrease. Fortunately, dBase III Plus provides a command which searches at a rate many times faster than the LIST or LOCATE command. The command is called FIND. To use this command, your database must be indexed and you may only search based on the indexed field.

1. USE the file created in Part A.

2. INDEX ON POPULATION TO POP.

3. FIND and print the city with a population of 43,900 by typing:

>   FIND 43900 <RET>
>
>   DISPLAY TO PRINT <RET>

4. Find and print the cities with the following populations:

            491,800
             58,000
            143,900

5. Use the original database. Index the file based on the city
field. Find and print the following city records:

            TriCities
            Everett
            Yakima

*************************** R E P O R T S ***************************

EXERCISE 7

Direct Mailing List

Commands used:	CREATE
	USE
	LIST
	CREATE LABEL
	MODIFY LABEL
	LABEL FORM

Level of difficulty: [2]

Type of application: [Marketing]

Purpose: One of the most practical applications for a database is a mail label generator. Once you have entered names and addresses in a database, it is possible to generate them as mailing labels. Even more importantly, you can arrange your label printing by such criteria as State, City, or Zip Code.

PROBLEM:

The mail order business for computer software is very competitive. As a small business owner and programmer, you have managed to do quite well in marketing a program that advises individuals on personal financial matters. You have used a popular computer magazine to advertise the software.

Now, however, you are faced with a problem. You have just completed a revision of your program and wish to announce the new version to past customers. You wish to offer the update to previous buyers for only a small portion of the program's original price.

ANALYSIS:

A letter has been drafted to announce this special offer, but it must be sent to thousands of users. Although you could have your secretary type the address of each user on an envelope, you have opted to create a database and print the mailing labels. This will allow you to do other direct mailings with a minimum of effort.

DEVELOPMENT:

Part A

1.   Your first job will be to create a database and fill it with
the names and addresses listed in FIGURE 7.2.   (This is a partial
list of your customers and will suffice to test your idea.)   Use
the file structure in FIGURE 7.1 to create the database.

---

field name	type	width	dec
LNAME	C	10	
FNAME	C	15	
ADDRESS	C	25	
CITY	C	15	
STATE	C	2	
ZIP	C	10	

FIGURE 7.1

2.   When you are finished creating the database, elect to
immediately enter the records in FIGURE 7.2.

```
Johnson                        Burger
George                         Bill
W. 2222 Catiplar Lane          N. 999 Hamburger Grove
Nome                           French Fry
AK                             AK
34789                          11111

Hatton                         Wonka
Roy                            Willy
S. 6785 Mountain View          W. 5555 Chocolate Dr.
Musk                           Spokane
MN                             WA
67892                          99207

Bonzo                          Conan
Ron                            Barbarian
W.   345 Washington            N. 22 Cimmera
Spokane                        Castle
WA                             FL
99207                          67676
```

FIGURE 7.2

3. Once the database is complete, INDEX it based on ZIP field. (The Post Office requires bulk mailings to be grouped based on Zip Code.)

4. At the dot prompt, type:

> CREATE LABEL   <RET>

5. When dBase III Plus prompts for a file name, type:

> LABEL   <RET>

6. dBase III Plus will display the screen shown in FIGURE 7.3.

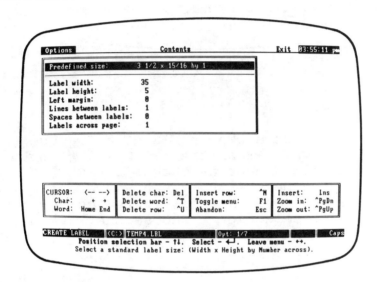

FIGURE 7.3

7. You can change any of the parameters on the screen to modify the appearance of your labels. Printers print a standard 10 characters to the inch (CPI) across the page and 6 lines to the inch.

8. Since you do not want to make any changes for the present, just press the right arrow key to move the highlighted cursor at the top of the screen to the CONTENTS selection and press <RET>. Notice that the display changes to display the Label Entry screen shown in FIGURE 7.4.

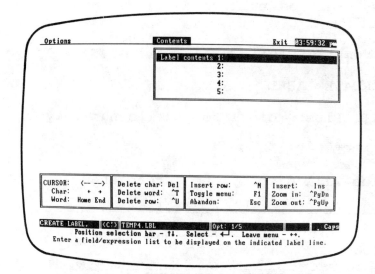

FIGURE 7.4

10. Enter the information shown in FIGURE 7.5. Use the arrow
keys to move up and down. Press the <RET> key to select a line
for entry. Type the field name as shown in FIGURE 7.5. Press
<RET> to move on to the next line. When you are finished, use
your right arrow key to move the highlighted cursor at the top of
the screen to the EXIT selection. Choose the SAVE option by
using your arrow keys and the <RET> key.

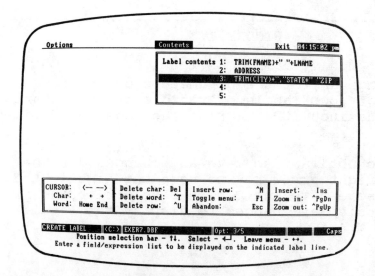

FIGURE 7.5

The TRIM command shown in front of FNAME and CITY is used to trim off the blank spaces that dBase III Plus adds to the contents of each field. The +", "+ puts a comma and blank space between CITY and STATE, so they like this: **Spokane, Wa.** If you need to make changes in your label format, you can use the MODIFY LABEL command. It functions just like the CREATE LABEL command.

11. When the dot prompt appears, you can print your labels by typing:

        LABEL FORM label TO PRINT   <RET>

Part B

1. Use the database created in Part A.

2. SET INDEX TO ZIP.

3. You now want to print just the mailing labels for the Zip Code 99207. To do this, type:

        LABEL FORM label FOR zip = '99207' TO PRINT   <RET>

4. Print just the mailing labels for Spokane.

5. Print the mailing label for George Johnson.

Part C

1. Use the database created in Part A.

2. SET INDEX TO ZIP.

3. You can print the first three labels in your database by typing:

        GO TOP <RET>

        LABEL FORM MAIL NEXT 3 TO PRINT   <RET>

4. Print the first four labels in your database.

EXERCISE 8

Travel Expense Report

Commands used: CREATE
                  USE
                  LIST
                  CREATE REPORT
                  MODIFY REPORT
                  REPORT FORM
                  INDEX

Level of difficulty: [2]

Type of application: [Accounting]

Purpose: The report generator, built into dBase III Plus, allows you to construct column reports. You will use this generator to create a column report with subtotals.

PROBLEM:

You have just started keeping track of your travel expenses by entering them in a dBase III Plus file. (See FIGURE 8.1.) You use the first three fields in your database to record the type, amount, and date of the expense. The next two fields record the payee and where the transaction occurred. The last field contains the details of the transaction.

CATEGORY	AMOUNT	DATE	PAYEE	AREA	MEMO
Room	$ 56.00	10/18/87	Motel YYY	Portland	
Meal	$ 44.00	10/18/87	Dent's Mush	Portland	
Gas	$ 21.00	10/18/87	Qix Gas	Portland	
Room	$ 40.22	10/19/87	Fast 6 Inn	Seattle	
Gas	$ 22.00	10/19/87	Union 36	Seattle	
Meal	$ 34.88	10/19/87	Mr. Beef	Seattle	
Meal	$ 45.90	10/20/87	Uncle Wicks	Spokane	
Room	$120.00	10/20/87	Top Hat Inn	Spokane	

FIGURE 8.1

You can already see that, as your database grows, it will be difficult to determine how much you are spending on specific expense categories. For instance, you might want to know how much you have spent on hotel rooms or meals. You could use the dBase III Plus command TOTAL, introduced in Exercise 5, to produce subtotals based on individual expense categories. This command, however, simply combines like entries to arrive at subtotals and fails to list the separate records that comprise the subtotal. You want to be able to see these records grouped together with their accompanying subtotals.

In addition to your need to subtotal the expense report by category, you would also like to create a second subtotal. This subsubtotal would divide each expense category into subgroups based on the date of the expense.

ANALYSIS:

Fortunately, dBase III Plus provides a report generator which groups records by any field and displays a subtotal when appropriate. The generator will even allow you to have a second level of grouping based on another field.

Another major advantage of the REPORT command is its ability to organize data into pages. Unlike the LIST command, which continually displays records until the end of the file is reached, the REPORT command pauses at the end of each page for you to examine the information.

A major drawback of the column report generator is its 80 character screen width. As a result, the fields in your column report can total no more than 80 characters. This limit can be exceeded when printing by using the compressed mode or a wide carriage printer. However, you are still limited to displaying only 80 characters on your screen. Reports involving fields totaling more than 80 characters are often best handled by custom screens. (Custom screen construction will be covered in the exercises dealing with command files.)

Since the fields in your database total less than 80 characters (minus the MEMO field), you will be able to use the REPORT command to create specialized reports detailing your expense activity.

Before you start, there is an important rule to keep in mind when using the REPORT command: **always index or sort the field you wish to group on.** If you fail to do this, the generator may not group the records correctly. The report generator looks at each record consecutively and will continue to group like entries until it encounters a different entry. For example, FIGURE 8.1 on page 36 shows records for meal expenses in several places. If you were to create a report grouped on the CATEGORY field, without sorting or indexing the field, you would end up with two subtotals for meal expense.

DEVELOPMENT:

Part A

1. Create a database using the file structure listed in FIGURE 8.2 and name it TRAVEL.

Field Name	Type	Width	Dec
CATEGORY	Character	20	
AMOUNT	Numeric	8	2
DATE	Date	8	
PAYEE	Character	20	
AREA	Character	10	
MEMO	Memo	10	

FIGURE 8.2

2. Enter the records shown in FIGURE 8.1 on page 36. (Assume that the details for the memo field have already been entered.)

3. At the dot prompt, type:

            CREATE REPORT <RET>

            TRAVEL <RET>

4. The screen in FIGURE 8.3 will appear. This screen lists the report format options. The <F1> function key will cause the lower part of the screen to display either a help window or a picture of the report as you define it.

The default settings are sufficient for present purposes, so changes are unnecessary. However, you do wish to title this report, so with the "Page title" highlighted, press the <RET> key and type:

            Travel Expense Report <RET>
            Based on Category and Date of Expense <RET>

When you finish with the title, continue pressing the <RET> key
until the side bar disappears.

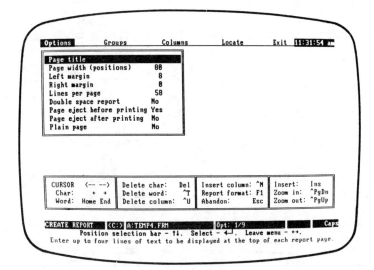

FIGURE 8.3

5. Use the right arrow key to select the "Groups" option from
the top menu. The screen depicted in FIGURE 8.4 will appear.
Press the <RET> key to select the "Group on expression" option
from the submenu. This selection will tell dBase III Plus which
field to group on. Type:

CATEGORY <RET>

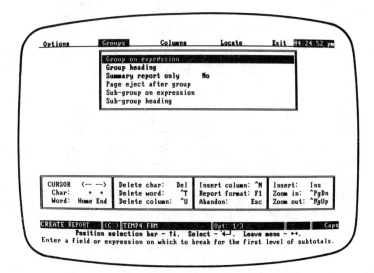

FIGURE 8.4

6. Now press the down arrow key to select the "Group heading"
option. You want to title each group "Type of Expense," so type:

TYPE OF EXPENSE <RET>

7. Move the highlight down to the "Sub-group on expression"
option and type:

DATE <RET>

This will cause dBase to subsubtotal on the DATE field.

8. Give the sub-group the heading of "DATE OF EXPENSE."

9. Use the right arrow key to select the Columns option from the
top menu. The display in FIGURE 8.5 will appear.

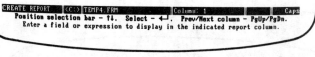

FIGURE 8.5

Notice that the bottom of the screen indicates which column of
the report you are working on. You can enter any field name from
your database at this point. After pressing <RET>, the F10 key
will cause a list of the fields in your database to appear in the
left corner of your screen. You can use the arrow keys and <RET>
key to select a field. When you enter a field name, dBase III
Plus will automatically display the width of the field in the sub
menu next to the "Width" prompt. If the field is a Numeric type,
you can specify the number of decimal places to be displayed by
entering a number next to the "Decimal places" prompt. The last
prompt in the sub menu allows you to total on this column.

10. Press the F10 key and select the CATEGORY field.

11. Press the <PgDn> key to move to the next column of the report.

12. Press F10 and choose the AMOUNT field. (Notice that dBase assumes you want to total on this Numeric field.)

13. Move to the next column and select the PAYEE field.

14. For the last column of the report, choose the AREA field.

15. Now use the right arrow key to move the cursor to the Exit option. Press <RET> to save your report.

16. To display your report, type:

           REPORT FORM travel <RET>

Look a bit strange? Why do you think you have so many duplicate subtotals? The answer is simple; you have not indexed the file yet.

17. INDEX ON category TO report1 <RET>

18. Display the report.

19. To print a copy of the report, type:

           REPORT FORM travel TO PRINT <RET>

Part B

1. If you QUIT after the last section, USE the database created in Part A.

2. Create a report grouped by DATE. Include the first five fields of your database.

3. Print the report.

************** M U L T I P L E   D A T A B A S E S ************

EXERCISE 9

Sales Manager

Commands used:	CREATE
	USE
	LIST
	JOIN
	SORT
	CREATE REPORT
	COPY

Level of difficulty: [3]

Type of application: [Management]

Purpose: This exercise illustrates the power of dBase III Plus to join two databases.

PROBLEM:

You have been using a dBase III Plus file to keep track of your customers and their year-to-date sales.   FIGURE 9.1 shows a partial listing from this database.

CUSTNO	CUSTNAME	YTDSALES
101	John Thompson	$650.00
105	Bill Smith	$625.00
103	Phil Jones	$550.00
106	Jean Simmons	$400.00
102	Mary Ann Wilson	$ 50.00
104	Terry Loll	$700.00

FIGURE 9.1

Another database contains your salespeople and their territories. FIGURE 9.2 contains several records from this file.

CUSTNO	SALESPER	CITY
103	Lisa Jinks	Sacramento
106	Sue Smith	Portland
104	Lisa Jinks	Sacramento
101	Sue Smith	Portland
102	Sue Smith	Portland

FIGURE 9.2

You want to determine how much each saleperson has sold, but the year-to-date sales figures are in one database while the sales people are in another.

ANALYSIS:

It is unusual to find any single database containing sufficient detail to satisfy every user inquiry. Often the data needed to answer a particular query will reside in two or more databases. Foreseeing this situation, dBase III Plus provides the means to combine information from separate files. The JOIN command allows you to create a new file which contains selected data from two existing databases. Two files can be joined when they share a common field. The width and type of a common field must be identical in both files. Notice that the CUSTNO field appears in both of the databases discussed above. Due to careful planning, this field has the same structure in both files.

When two files are joined, only those records which share matching data in their common field will be placed in the new database. Thus, data in the common field must be limited to unique values. If values are repeated, it will be uncertain as to which records will arrive in the new file. Again, as a result of your foresight for the need to join the above two files, their common field contains only unique customer numbers.

The first step in preparing a report with year-to-date sales totals for each salesperson is to get the necessary data into one database. You can accomplish this task by joining the two files illustrated in FIGURES 9.1 and 9.2. This will create a new database which contains both your sales people and their sales. Finally, you will use the report generator to group records based on SALESPER and subtotaled on YTDSALES to produce the required report.

DEVELOPMENT:

Part A

1. Create two file structures for the records in FIGURE 9.1 and 9.2. Name the first database CUST and the second SALES. Be sure to use the same width and type in both databases for the CUSTNO field.

2. Enter the records listed in FIGURE 9.1 and 9.2. (These records will suffice to test your solution.)

3. Type:

                    CLEAR ALL   <RET>

to close all open files.

4. Joining the files in the most efficient manner will require you to sort them on their common field. Type the following:

> USE cust <RET>
>
> SORT ON custno TO temp <RET>
>
> USE temp <RET>
>
> Y   (To overwrite the temp.dbf file.)
>
> COPY TO cust <RET>
>
> Y   (To overwrite the cust.dbf file.)

5. Next to sort the sales file, type:

> USE sales <RET>
>
> SORT ON custno TO temp <RET>
>
> USE temp <RET>
>
> COPY TO sales <RET>
>
> Y   (To overwrite the sales.dbf file.)

6. With both files sorted on their common field, you can now use the JOIN command. This command requires that you first select a primary database and then a secondary file. The secondary file will need a separate memory space. The SELECT command provides this memory space and the letters A-J provide names for the memory partitions. The first memory space you have been working in has the default name of A.   Type:

> USE cust <RET>
>
> SELECT b <RET>
>
> USE sales <RET>

7. The JOIN command can be issued at this point. The file name COMBINE will be the name of the new database created by this command. The FOR condition specifies the fields used to join the two databases on. Notice the "b->" symbol. This symbol tells dBase that the second field name belongs to the database in partition B. The FIELDS extension to the command allows you to specify which fields are to be included in the new database. Now type:

  JOIN TO combine FOR custno=b->custno FIELDS salesper,ytdsales

8. USE combine.

9. Print a copy of the new database's structure and records.

Part B

1. USE the new file created in Part A.

2. With the help of the report generator, print a report grouped by salesperson.

Part C

1. CLEAR ALL files.

2. JOIN the cust and sales files to produce a new file with the fields city and ytdsales.

3. Print a report grouped by city.

EXERCISE 10

Inventory Tracking

Commands used:	CREATE
	USE
	LIST
	UPDATE
	SORT
	INDEX
	LIST STRUCTURE TO PRINT

Level of difficulty: [2]

Type of application: [Accounting]

Purpose: This problem demonstrates dBase III Plus's ability to update a master file from a transaction file.

PROBLEM:

FIGURE 10.1 illustrates a partial listing from your inventory file. Use this master file to keep track of inventory levels and order quantities. (Such matters as vendor addresses, item costs, on-order status, and model numbers are stored in another related file.)

ITEMNO	DESCRIPTION	QUANTITY
100006	floppy disk drive	30
100004	internal modem	23
100001	XY-computer	10
100002	printer	18
100003	wide carriage printer	20
100005	hard disk drive	15

FIGURE 10.1

During the course of a business day, you make numerous sales. FIGURE 10.2 lists several of these transactions. Each evening, you edit your master file to reflect the inventory changes caused by the day's sales. This is a very time consuming process.

ITEMNO	CUSTOMER	QUANTITY	PRICE
100005	Robert's Computers	2	359.00
100001	Computer Spot	3	899.00
100003	The Computer Edge	5	600.00
100004	Computer Spot	4	150.00
100006	Bits & Bytes	1	90.00

FIGURE 10.2

ANALYSIS:

When business transactions are numerous and uniform in nature
(like sales or payroll), they are often best handled in a batch
rather than individually. dBase III Plus provides a command
which greatly expedites batch processing. The UPDATE command
will change the information in a master file based on the data in
a transaction file. In other words, you can create a sales
database and use it to update your master inventory file.
Changes to inventory levels will be made all at once, rather than
one at a time with the EDIT command.

Like the JOIN command from the last exercise, the UPDATE command
requires a shared field between the transaction and master files.
In this exercise, the common field is ITEMNO. Unlike the common
field from Exercise 9, you will notice that ITEMNO has repeating
values. This is allowable when using the UPDATE command. For
example, in one day, you may sell 5 products with the same item
number. When updating, each sale's transaction will simply
subtract one item from the inventory quantity on hand.

Since the UPDATE command introduces the potential for quick and
vast changes, it also brings about the possibility of extensive
damage. For instance, if mistakes are present in your
transaction file, they will corrupt your master file when you
update. A policy of backing up your master file before updating,
will reduce the chances for mishap. FIGURE 10.3 illustrates this
concept.

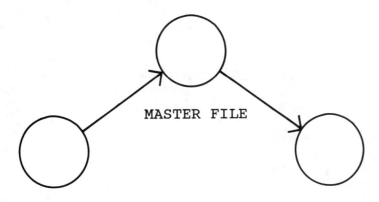

MASTER FILE

TRANSACTION FILE   OLD MASTER FILE

FIGURE 10.3

DEVELOPMENT:

Part A

1. Create two databases from the information provided in FIGURES 10.1 and 10.2. Name the first file MASTER and the second TRANS.

2. Enter the records shown in the above figures in their respective files.

3. The transaction file must be sorted before proceeding further, so type:

        USE trans   <RET>

        SORT ON itemno TO temp   <RET>

        USE temp   <RET>

        COPY TO trans   <RET>

        Y   (To overwrite the trans.dbf file.)

4. To protect your master file type:

        USE master   <RET>

        COPY TO oldmast   <RET>

You now have a backup file if something goes wrong.

5. Although you may sort the master file, this process can use
up a great deal of disk storage. Instead, it is best to index
the master file. Type:

> USE master <RET>
>
> INDEX ON itemno TO itemno <RET>
>
> SELECT b <RET>
>
> USE trans <RET>
>
> SELECT a <RET>

6. Now you can update the quantity level in the master file from
the quantity sold in the transaction file.

> UPDATE ON itemno FROM b REPLACE quantity WITH;
> quantity - b->quantity <RET>

6. Print a copy of the updated records in your master file.

Part B

1. FIGURE 10.4 contains the next day's sales. Update the master
file again.

ITEMNO	CUSTOMER	QUANTITY	PRICE
100002	The Computer Place	2	$400.00
100005	Computer Spot	1	$359.00
100006	The Computer Edge	5	$ 90.00
100004	Bits & Bytes	4	$150.00

FIGURE 10.4

2. Print the records from the updated master file.

******************** C O M M A N D   F I L E S ******************

EXERCISE 11

Cash Disbursements Journal

Commands used:

CREATE	SET TALK ON/OFF	SORT
DO <filename>	SET DEFAULT TO B	STORE
RETURN	SET BELL OFF	SAY
DO CASE/ENDCASE	SET FORMAT TO	APPEND
DO WHILE/ENDDO	GO TOP/BOTTOM	READ
IF<condition>/ENDIF	CLEAR	UPPER(memvar>
USE	WAIT	SUM
AVERAGE	VAL(memvar)	MODIFY COMMAND

Level of difficulty: [3]

Type of application: [Accounting]

Purpose: The true power of dBase III Plus can only be realized by employing command files. These files allow the user to build complete menu driven applications. This exercise demonstrates just such a system. Additionally, the advantages of a structured approach to creating command files is stressed.

PROBLEM:

You have been using dBase to keep track of the checks written for your company. FIGURE 11.1 shows the structure of this cash disbursements database.

At the end of the month, you use this database to create a budget report detailing the amounts spent on each expense category. The field CATEGORY is the key to producing this monthly report. It provides the means to total expenses by type. You use the TOTAL command to group and subtotal all your records based on the field CATEGORY.

Field Name	Type	Width	Dec
CATEGORY	Character	10	
CHECK	Character	5	
AMOUNT	Numeric	10	2
DATE	Date	8	
PAYTO	Character	20	
FOR	Character	25	

FIGURE 11.1

FIGURE 11.2 illustrates a partial listing of the records in your database.

CATEGORY	CHECK	AMOUNT	DATE	PAYTO	FOR
UTIL	101	90.00	01/02/87	N. W. Bell	phone
UTIL	104	76.00	01/15/87	WWP	electric
OFF	102	200.00	01/08/87	Bud's Supply	cabinet
RENT	109	500.00	01/25/87	John's Realty	Feb. rent
OFF	103	34.45	01/10/87	Bud's Supply	desk
MISC	112	23.33	02/03/87	City Treasurer	bus. Lic.
PRINT	134	45.90	02/14/87	Qix	printing

FIGURE 11.2

The time required to record expenses and prepare reports has become unacceptable. You would like to turn the task over to your bookkeeper but she is untrained in dBase III Plus operations.

ANALYSIS:

The answer is clear. You need to create a command file(s) which provides the bookkeeper with a menu and walks her through entering, finding, and reporting data. This way, she can use the system without prior training or knowledge of dBase III Plus.

There are seven basic steps in developing a successful dBase III Plus application. These steps will be explained step-by-step on pp. 54-60.

1.   Define your information requirements.

2.   Break the job into its logical components.

3.   Write out, in English-like sentences, how each component or routine will achieve its objectives. (This process is often referred to as pseudocoding.)

4.   Based on the pseudocoding, write the actual dBase III Plus commands or instructions for each routine.

5.   Test each routine upon completion.

6.   Link the routines together with the main driver routine.

7.   Test the complete system to see if it meets the original objectives of the project.

I.   INFORMATION OBJECTIVES DEFINED

You currently use the cash disbursement database to store
information about the checks you write. Once a month you total
expenses by budget category to evaluate where your firm's funds
are being expended. From time to time, you also need to locate a
particular check by number, date, or budget category.

After a careful analysis of your information needs, you arrive at
the following objectives for your application:

1.   The system should provide a means for entering check
     information.

2.   The system should allow the user to locate records based on
     check number, date, and budget category.

3.   The system should produce, upon request, a report grouped
     and subtotaled by budget category.

4.   The entire system should be menu driven for ease of use.

II. BREAKING THE SYSTEM INTO LOGICAL COMPONENTS

This approach is often referred to as a top-down design. You
first examine the overall job to be done and then break it into
its logical parts. This gives you a top-down perspective of the
entire project. Separating a job into subroutines allows you to
work on smaller more easily understood segments. The cash
disbursement system can be broken into these components:

1.   A subroutine to prompt the user to enter check
     information;

2.   A subroutine to search the database by check
     number, date, and budget category;

3.   A subroutine to group and subtotal records by budget
     category;

4.   A driver routine to link all of the above routines together
     and provide the user with a menu of options.

III. PSEUDOCODING

Writing down, step by step, how each module or subroutine is to
accomplish its task has several advantages. First, it provides a
map for creating the actual command files. Second, and just as
important, it acts as documentation for the command file. This
documentation can prove invaluable in trouble-shooting or
modifying the file at a later date.

The pseudocode for each of the four command files necessary to implement the cash disbursement system is listed below. The first listing is for the data entry subroutine.

1.   Pseudocode for the Entry Command File:

Clear the display.
Do the following while the user wishes to enter another record.
     Clear the screen again.
     Open a new record.
     Display the record's fields using a predefined entry screen.
     Add any data entered in the screen to the new record.
     Ask the user if he wishes to add another record.
Loop back up.
Return to the main menu of options.

2.   Pseudocode for the Search Command File:

Clear the screen.
Use the database EXPENSE.
Do the following while the user wishes to continue searching.
     Display a screen of possible fields to search on.
     Ask the user to choose a field to search by.
     Ask the user to enter a match for the field chosen.
     Search for the match.
     If a match is found, display it.
     If no match is found, inform the user.
     In either case, ask the user if he wishes to search again.
Loop back up.
Return to the main menu of options.

3.   Pseudocode for the Report Command File:

Clear the screen.
Organize the database on the CATEGORY field.
Check to see if the report should be printed or displayed.
Use a predefined report form to group and subtotal records based on the expense category.
Return to the main menu of options.

4. Pseudocode for the Menu Command File:

Clear the screen.
Turn off the beeping sound associated with dBase III Plus data
entry.
Use the database EXPENSE.
Do the following while the user continues.
     Display a menu of these options:
     (1) Check entry
     (2) Check search
     (3) Monthly expense report
     (4) Leave the application
     Based on the user's selection, implement the proper
     subroutine.
Loop back up.
Notify the user that the program is terminated.

IV. **WRITING THE ACTUAL INSTRUCTIONS (CODE)**

Writing an understandable and maintainable command file requires
a structured approach. A command file is simply a set of dBase
III Plus instructions designed to accomplish some task.
Organizing these instructions properly requires the use of
Control Structures. Control Structures act as traffic cops,
directing the flow of logic in a command file. This flow of
control forces the command file to execute instructions in a
clear pattern and not skip randomly about. There are three types
of Control Structures:

     1.   Sequencing
     2.   Selection
     3.   Iteration (looping)

Sequencing is the orderly flow of logic from one command to the
next. In a command file, this involves the execution of one
instruction after another. When dBase completes an instruction
on one line, it will then move to the line below and carry out
the next command. This progression continues until either the
end of the file is reached or another type of Control Structure
is encountered.

Selection is accomplished by the IF-THEN-ELSE command and CASE
statement in dBase III Plus. This Control Structure selects a
path of logic flow based on whether a conditional statement's
antecedent is true or false. A conditional statement is any IF-
THEN statement. The antecedent is the IF part of the statement.
For example,

```
IF answer="Y"        (antecedent)
   LIST TO PRINT     (This command will execute if answer="Y")
ELSE
   LIST              (This command will execute if answer<>"Y")
ENDIF
```

Iteration or looping is accomplished in dBase III Plus by the DO WHILE command. When this command is used, all the instructions contained within the DO WHILE and ENDO statements will repeat until the condition in the DO WHILE statement becomes false. For example,

```
DO WHILE .NOT. EOF()
    DISPLAY TO PRINT                (Each record in the file will be
ENDDO printing records             printed until the end-of-file
                                   EOF is reached.)
```

With a combination of these three Control Structures, you can create easily understood and maintainable command files. Execution of instructions flow from one Control Structure to the next, never jumping out of sequence. Each structure, in essence, represents a "block." When the instructions in one block are completed, the flow of control goes to the next block. Thus, changing or debugging a command file is made easier. You need not follow a "spaghetti like" trail of logic to detect errors or add new lines of code.

Listed below are the actual command files for the cash disbursement system: (The first file is actually a custom screen file and is labeled so by the FMT extension.)

SCREEN.FMT

```
@  2, 27 SAY 'MONTHLY EXPENSE REPORT'
@  4,  5 SAY 'Amount of check: ' GET amount
@  4, 34 SAY 'Check number: ' GET check
@  6,  5 SAY 'Date of check: ' GET date
@  6, 34 SAY 'Paid to whom: ' GET payto
@  8,  5 SAY 'Explanation for funds expenditure: ' GET for
@ 10,  5 SAY 'Enter a selection from below: ' GET category
@ 12,  5 SAY 'Utilites=UTIL   Rent=RENT   Office supplies=OFF'
@ 14,  5 SAY 'Printing=PRINT  Misc.=MISC  '
```

ENTRY.PRG

```
CLEAR
SET INDEX TO CATEGORY
*  initial variable
STORE 'Y' TO pick
*  main processing loop
DO WHILE UPPER(pick)='Y'
    CLEAR
    APPEND BLANK
    SET FORMAT TO screen
    READ
    SET FORMAT TO
    @ 20,  5 SAY 'Enter another record? (Y/N) ' GET pick
```

```
    READ
ENDDO
RETURN
SEARCH.PRG


CLEAR
SET TALK OFF
*  initialize variables
STORE 0 TO select
STORE 'Y' TO entry
DO WHILE UPPER(entry)='Y'
    CLEAR
    *  search menu
    @  5, 15 SAY 'MENU FOR SEARCHING FILE'
    @ 10,  7 SAY '1) Search by CHECK NUMBER'
    @ 11,  7 SAY '2) Search by DATE OF CHECK'
    @ 12,  7 SAY '3) Search by BUDGET CATEGORY'
    @ 14,  7 SAY '=============================='
    @ 20,  5 SAY 'Enter a number--> ' GET select
    READ
    DO CASE
        CASE select=1
            STORE 'CHECK' to fieldname
        CASE select=2
            STORE 'DTOC(DATE)' to fieldname
        CASE select=3
            STORE 'AMOUNT' TO fieldname
    ENDCASE
    CLEAR
    STORE '                              ' TO key
    @ 10, 10 SAY 'Now type the entry to search for ' GET key
    READ
    STORE TRIM(key) TO key
    CLEAR
    @ 10, 10 say 'SEARCHING FOR RECORDS'
    LOCATE FOR UPPER(&fieldname)=UPPER(key)
    DO WHILE .NOT. EOF()
        CLEAR
        SET FORMAT TO screen
        READ
        SET FORMAT TO
        CLEAR
        STORE 'Y' TO decision
        @ 10, 10 SAY 'CONTINUE SEARCH (Y/N) ' GET decision
        READ
        IF UPPER(decision)='N'
            GO BOTTOM
        ENDIF
        CONTINUE
    ENDDO
    CLEAR
    @ 10, 10 SAY 'END OF FILE REACHED'
    @ 12, 10 SAY 'ANOTHER SEARCH (Y/N) ' GET entry
    READ
```

```
ENDDO
SET TALK ON
RETURN
REPORT.PRG


CLEAR
SET TALK OFF
SET INDEX TO CATEGORY
*  initialize variables
STORE ' ' TO selection
*  check report, grouped by type of expense
@ 10, 10 SAY 'PRINT THE REPORT? (Y/N) ' GET selection
READ
IF UPPER(selection) = 'Y'
    SET PRINT ON
ENDIF
REPORT FORM total
WAIT
SET PRINT OFF
SET TALK OFF
RETURN


MENU.PRG


CLEAR
SET TALK OFF
SET BELL OFF
USE expense
*  initialize variable
STORE 1 TO choice
*  main processing loop
DO WHILE choice<>4
    CLEAR
    @  1, 20 SAY 'CASH DISBURSEMENT JOURNAL'
    @  5, 28 SAY 'MAIN MENU'
    @ 10,  5 SAY '1) Check Entry Screen'
    @ 11,  5 SAY '2) Search Routine'
    @ 12,  5 SAY '3) Report by Expense Category'
    @ 13,  5 SAY '4) Quit'
    @ 20,  5
    INPUT 'Enter a number--> ' TO choice
    DO CASE
        CASE choice=1
            DO entry
        CASE choice=2
            DO search
        CASE choice=3
            DO report
    ENDCASE
ENDDO
CLEAR
SET TALK ON
@  10, 10 SAY 'MENU PROGRAM TERMINATED'
```

V.   TESTING A COMMAND FILE

You test a command file by using it for its intended purpose.
Try to think of all the situations that may occur when using the
file and try them.   When errors do occur, there are procedures
to help eliminate them.   The first step in finding an error is to
realize what type of error has occurred.

There are two types of command file errors:

> 1.   Syntax -- misspelling or improper use of commands
> 2.   Logic -- misuse of a command

Syntax errors are the most common and easily fixed.   There are a
few simple guidelines for spotting syntax errors:

> ** Check for incorrect spellings of dBase commands
> ** Check for improper or missing command parameters
>   (e.g. SET DEFAULT B --- the "TO" is missing)

Logic errors occur because a command file instruction asks dBase
III Plus to perform an action contrary to the user's desires.
Several steps can be taken to correct this type of error:

> ** Recheck pseudocode logic to make sure it is correct
> ** Recheck the actual instructions to make sure they
>   comply with the pseudo code

VII. TESTING THE COMPLETE SYSTEM

Testing the system as a whole involves checking for a proper
transfer of control from one subroutine to another.   This is a
fairly straightforward process.   You simply start the menu
command file and select and test each module to see if the system
works as it was originally designed to do.

DEVELOPMENT:

Part A

1.   CREATE a database using the structure provided in FIGURE 11.1
on page 52.   Name it EXPENSE.

2.   CREATE a report form based on the CATEGORY field.   Name it
TOTAL and title it "Report by Expense Category."   Include only
the CATEGORY and AMOUNT fields in your report.

3.   Using MODIFY COMMAND, create the command files listed in the
ANALYSIS section of this exercise.   (Be sure to use the file
extension FMT when creating the screen format file.)

4. Test and debug the ENTRY command file by entering the records from FIGURE 11.2. Next, index the records based on the CATEGORY field to an index file called "category." as you complete it.

5. Test and debug the SEARCH command file by searching for check number 101.

6. Test and debug the REPORT command file by printing the expense report.

7. Test and debug the whole system.

8. Print a listing of each command file by typing:

>   SET PRINT ON <RET>

>   TYPE <file name>.* <RET> (Repeat this for each file.)

>   SET PRINT OFF <RET>

Part B

1. Modify the system developed in Part A to produce a second report grouped and subtotaled on the DATE field. This report should display only the CATEGORY and AMOUNT fields. (Be sure to add the new command file option to the menu program and index the database by date.)

2. Print the new report. Also print a listing of your new command file and the altered menu file.

Contents

EXERCISE 1

Direct Mail

Commands used: OPENING MENU:

L -- change logged disk drive
D -- open a document file
P -- print a document

MAIN MENU:

<CTRL> S -- move cursor one
            character to the left
<CTRL> D -- move cursor one
            character to the right
<CTRL> A -- move cursor one word
            to the left
<CTRL> F -- move cursor one word
            to the right
<CTRL> E -- move cursor up one
            line
<CTRL> V -- move cursor down one
            line
<CTRL> G -- delete the character
            that the cursor is
            sitting on
<CTRL> N -- insert a line

BLOCK MENU:
<CTRL> K to bring up Block Menu

<CTRL> KD -- save document and
             return to Opening Menu

NOTE: <CTRL> may be represented by the symbol ^. For
example ^N

Level of difficulty: [1]

Purpose: This exercise covers the basics of
          opening a document and entering
          text.

PROBLEM:

Your first day on the job at the Exotic Travel Agency has
been an exciting one. Your boss has decided to try a new
marketing strategy to attract repeat business. She wants to

make a special travel offer to the firm's current clientele. A direct mailer will be used to announce this new travel offer and you have been asked to type this promotional letter. A draft of the letter is shown in FIGURE 1.1

ANALYSIS:

Your employer has requested this letter be typed in standard letter format. This entails using one-inch left and right margins and vertical centering of text from top to bottom. WordStar's default settings automatically provide one-inch side margins with a page length of 55 lines of text. Since the margins are preset at one inch, all that remains for you to do is to center the text vertically on the page. To do this, you first type the document; then count the number of lines of text. Subtract the total lines of text from 55 and divide by two to find the number of blank lines for each margin. For instance, if a letter takes 45 lines, then the top and bottom margins should be 5 lines each (55-45= 10 lines and 10/2= 5 lines each.)

DEVELOPMENT:

Part A

1. Use L from the Opening Menu to change the logged disk drive. Enter the letter of the drive to be used for document storage.

2. Use D in the Opening Menu to create a new document named **EXOTIC.**

3. Do not change the default margin settings.

4. Make sure that the indicator, in the upper-right corner of the screen displays "INSERT ON". If not, hold down the <CTRL> key and press V (^V) to activate it. Keyboard the letter in FIGURE 1.1.

5. Proofread the document. If you made keyboarding errors, use the cursor movement keys and delete keys (listed in the Main Menu) to correct the mistake(s).

6. To center the text vertically, move the cursor to the last line of the letter. The top of your screen shows the document name and the cursor position by vertical line and horizontal column number. The line number is an easy way to discover the total lines in your document. This saves you the time-consuming task of counting lines. Subtract the total number of lines from 55 and divide by two to find the top and bottom margins. Move the cursor to line 1 of your document and hold down the <CTRL> key and press N(^N) to

insert the necessary blank lines for the proper top margin. If the top margin was calculated correctly, the bottom margin will be correct.

7. Hold down the <CTRL> key and press K(^K) to bring up the Block Menu and press the letter D to save the document.

8. After the document is saved, you are back to the Opening Menu. To print the document, make sure the printer is ON LINE, press P and you will be asked to enter the name of the file to print. Enter EXOTIC and press the <ESC> key.

Dear Patron:

    As a valued customer of the Exotic Travel Agency, you are entitled to a special $599 travel package to Hawaii! This 7-day all expense paid vacation includes room, meals, and round-trip air fare. Now through December, this unbelievable package can be yours as a preferred customer of Exotic Travel.

    Imagine yourself walking along the beach at Waikiki watching a fantastic sunset or relaxing at one of the many fine restaurants on the main island while enjoying a wide variety of tropical delicacies. All of this can be yours for only $599!

    To take advantage of this offer, you must make your reservations two weeks in advance of passage. Call today to reserve a piece of paradise.

                                        Sincerely,

                                        Mary Smith
                                        President

                        FIGURE 1.1

Part B

When you submit the promotional letter to Ms. Smith for her signature, she decides to add the text shown in FIGURE 1.2.

1. Open the document named **EXOTIC**.

2. Move the cursor to the beginning of the last paragraph.
Use ^N to insert a blank line and keyboard the text in
FIGURE 1.2. After you finish keyboarding the paragraph,
press <RET> (or ENTER) to create a blank line.

3. Re-calculate and center the text vertically.

4. Save and print the document.

    As an added incentive, Exotic Travel will provide a
free deluxe rental car for all five days of your stay in
Hawaii. See the main island in the comfort and luxury of an
air conditioned sedan at no additional charge. We will even
pick up the bill for gas.

FIGURE 1.2

Part C

After eliciting suggestions from several of the office
travel agents, your boss asks you to enter a post script.

1. Open the document named **EXOTIC**.

2. Move the cursor to the end of the letter and use ^N to
insert two blank lines.

3. Keyboard the text in FIGURE 1.3.

4. Re-calculate and center the text vertically.

5. Save and print the letter.

P.S. If you make reservations for two or more, we will
reduce the package price to $499 per traveler! If you have
ever dreamed of going to Hawaii, now is the time to make
those dreams come true. This price may never happen again.
Plan today for an unforgettable vacation!

FIGURE 1.3

EXERCISE 2

Business Correspondence

Commands used: OPENING MENU:

L -- change logged disk drive
D -- open a document file
P -- print a document

MAIN MENU:

<CTRL> S -- move cursor one
            character to the left
<CTRL> D -- move cursor one
            character to the right
<CTRL> A -- move cursor one word
            to the left
<CTRL> F -- move cursor one word
            to the right
<CTRL> E -- move cursor up one
            line
<CTRL> V -- move cursor down one
            line
<CTRL> G -- delete the character
            that the cursor is
            sitting on
<CTRL> N -- insert a line
<CTRL> B -- reform text

BLOCK MENU:
<CTRL> K to bring up Block Menu

<CTRL> KD -- save document and
             return to Opening Menu

ONSCREEN MENU:
<CTRL> O to bring up Onscreen Menu

<CTRL> OL -- set left margin
<CTRL> OR -- set right margin
<CTRL> OJ -- turn On or Off
             Justification
<CTRL> OS -- set line spacing

NOTE: <CTRL> may be represented by the symbol ^. For
      example: ^N

Level of difficulty: [2]

Purpose: This exercise demonstrates a
number of WordStar's editing
capabilities.

PROBLEM:

You are a secretary/receptionist at Acme Outdoors. The
manager of the purchasing department has asked you to type
a letter as shown in FIGURE 2.1.

The letter is to be sent to the following address:

    Outrageous Distributors, Inc.
    1234 N.W. 56th Street
    Spokane, WA 99111

ANALYSIS:

The purchasing department manager has requested that the
letter be typed using block style. Since you have just
taken an Office Procedures class in college, you still
remember the nine essential parts that must appear in all
business letters. You also recall the basic rules for a
block style letter:

1. With block style, all letter parts begin at the left
margin.

2. Type the date two lines below the last line of the
letterhead.

3. The number of blank lines between the date and the
inside address may be adjusted so that the letter will be
centered vertically on the page.

4. The inside address is typed with at least three lines in
length.

5. One blank line goes between the inside address and the
salutation.

6. One blank line goes between the salutation and the body
of the letter. (Do not indent the paragraphs, always use one
blank line between paragraphs.)

7. One blank line between the body of the letter and the
complimentary close.

8. Allow at least three blank lines between the complimentary close and the typewritten signature (the name of the person signing the letter).

9. One blank line goes between the title or the typewritten signature and the reference initials of the typist.

DEVELOPMENT:

Part A

1. Open a new document named **LETTER**.

2. Following the rules for a block style letter, keyboard the document in FIGURE 2.1.

3. Save the document.

4. Print the document.

                                        August 12, 19x1

Gentlemen,

On July 1, I ordered a shipment of 35 sleeping bags to be delivered to San Jose on or before July 25. Your acknowledgment of the order dated July 8 indicated the order would be shipped in plenty of time to arrive here by July 25.

Today is August 12, and I still have not received the shipment. My customers need the sleeping bags desperately for their vacations. As you can understand, it is essential for me to supply my customers promptly since the selling season is very short.

                                        Sincerely,

                                        Mark Able

xx

                        FIGURE 2.1

Part B

After the purchasing manager reads your first draft, he thought the body of the letter might look better double spaced and with 50 characters on each line (left margin = 5, right margin = 55.) The manager also asked you to add the text shown in FIGURE 2.2 at the end of the second sentence of the last paragraph.

1.   Open the document named **LETTER**.

2.   Enter the text shown in FIGURE 2.2 at the end of the second paragraph.

3.   Hold down the <CTRL> key and press OL(^OL) and you will be asked to enter a left margin column number, enter 5.

4.   Hold down the <CTRL> key and press OR(^OR) to change the right margin to column 55.

5.   Move the cursor to the beginning of each line, hold down the <CTRL> key and press B(^B) to format the letter with the new margin settings.

6.   To double space the body of the letter, hold down the <CTRL> key and and press OS(^OS). You will be asked to enter a new line spacing (1-9), enter 2. At this point, you will see the indicator in the upper-right corner of the screen "LINE SPACING 2."

7.   Hold down the <CTRL> key and press O(^O). You have just called up the Onscreen Menu. If the menu shows that Justification is On, press J to turn it Off. If Justification is already off, press the SPACE BAR once to leave it unchanged and go back to the Main Menu.

8.   Move the cursor to the beginning of the first paragraph, hold down the <CTRL> key and press B(^B) to reformat the paragraph. If necessary, repeat this step until the paragraph is completely reformatted.

9.   Repeat step 8 for each remaining paragraph.

10. Save and print the letter.

Will you let me know if the order has been shipped and when I may expect to receive it? Please handle this matter immediately.

FIGURE 2.2

Part C

After seeing the second draft, the manager changes his mind
again; he likes the original margin settings and line
spacing. Also, the second paragraph is too long. He wants
to use the original format and start a new paragraph after
"...when I may expect to receive it."

1. Use ^OL and ^OR to change the margin settings back to 1
and 65.

2. Use ^OS to change the line spacing back to 1.

3. Move the cursor to the beginning of each line and use ^B
to reformat the entire letter.

4. Notice that the body of the letter is not right-
justified(blocked). This is because the Justification was
Off when you reformatted the text.

5. Use ^OJ to turn Justification On.

6. Format the body of the letter use ^B.

7. Move the cursor to the blank space after "...when I may
expect to receive it."   Press <RET> twice to start a new
paragraph and create a blank line.

8. Use ^B to format the new paragraph.

9. Save and print the letter.

EXERCISE 3

Interdepartmental Memorandum

Commands used: OPENING MENU:

       L -- change logged disk drive
       D -- open a document file
       P -- print a document

       MAIN MENU:

       <CTRL> S -- move cursor one
                   character to the left
       <CTRL> D -- move cursor one
                   character to the right
       <CTRL> A -- move cursor one word
                   to the left
       <CTRL> F -- move cursor one word
                   to the right
       <CTRL> E -- move cursor up one
                   line
       <CTRL> V -- move cursor down one
                   line
       <CTRL> G -- delete the character
                   that the cursor is
                   sitting on
       <CTRL> N -- insert a line

       BLOCK MENU:
       <CTRL> K to bring up Block Menu

       <CTRL> KD -- save the document and
                    return to the Opening
                    Menu
       <CTRL> KB -- begin block operations
       <CTRL> KK -- end block operations
       <CTRL> KY -- delete blocked text

       PRINT MENU:
       <CTRL> P to bring up Print Menu

       <CTRL> PB -- boldface printing
       <CTRL> PS -- underline text

       ONSCREEN MENU:
       <CTRL> O to bring up Onscreen Menu

       <CTRL> OC -- center text

NOTE: <CTRL> may be represented by the symbol ^. For
      example: ^N

Level of Difficulty: [2]

                    Purpose: This exercise illustrates a variety
                              of WordStar's print enhancing
                              features.

PROBLEM:

The controller, Joan Hayward, has requested that a
memorandum be keyboarded and sent to the Marketing
Department.

ANALYSIS:

Since the company is currently out of the preprinted office
memorandum forms, you will use WordStar to type the letter.
The basic rules for typing a memorandum on plain paper are
as follows:

1. The heading, MEMORANDUM, should be capitalized,
centered, and underlined.

2. Place two blank lines between the heading and the
guides.

3. The guides, TO, FROM, DATE, and SUBJECT, should be
capitalized, double spaced, and each followed by a colon.
Be sure to line up the colons.

4. Place three blank lines between the guides and the body
of the memorandum.

5. The body of the memorandum should be in block style and
single spaced.

6. Place one blank line between each paragraph.

DEVELOPMENT:

PART A

1. Open a new document named **MEMO**.

2. With INSERT ON, hold down the <CTRL> key and press
PS(^PS), then type: MEMORANDUM. Use ^PS again, immediately
following the word MEMORANDUM. The result should look like
this:

     ^SMEMORANDUM^S

3. To center the word MEMORANDUM, hold down the <CTRL> key
and press OC(^OC.)

4. Keyboard:

          To: Marketing Department
        From: Joan Hayward
        Date: August 23, 198x
     Subject: Budget Variances

5. Enter the memorandum in Figure 3.1 using the above
rules.

6. Save the document.

7. Print the document.

8. Check the printout against FIGURE 3.2.

It has come to my attention that several account executives
have exceeded their monthly expense budgets. Maintaining
these budgets is crucial to achieving our firm's long-term
objective of increased profit.

It is not my intention to become personally involved in the
decision-making process of the Marketing Department, but I
strongly suggest that every effort be made to stay within
budget limitations. If you feel your individual situation
warrants a change in your expense allotment, please contact
me. We will study the matter together.

The marketing director, Mr. Thompson, and I have spoken at
length concerning this topic, and we are in complete
agreement about the necessity of meeting budget parameters.

Thank you for your cooperation and effort in making this a
banner year for our organization.

                    FIGURE 3.1

<u>MEMORANDUM</u>

TO: Marketing Department

FROM: Joan Hayward

DATE: August 23, 198x

SUBJECT: Budget Variances

It has come to my attention that several account executives
have exceeded their monthly expense budgets. Maintaining
these budgets is crucial to achieving our firm's long-term
objective of increased profit.

It is not my intention to become personally involved in the
decision-making process of the Marketing Department, but I
strongly suggest that every effort be made to stay within
budget limitations. If you feel your individual situation
warrants a change in your expense allotment, please contact
me. We will study the matter together.

The marketing director, Mr. Thompson, and I have spoken at
length concerning this topic, and we are in complete
agreement about the necessity of meeting budget parameters.

Thank you for your cooperation and effort in making this a
banner year for our organization.

FIGURE 3.2

PART B

Ms. Hayward wants the subject "Budget Variance" to be
boldfaced and the last sentence of the second paragraph to
be deleted.

1. Open the document named **MEMO**.

2. With INSERT ON, move the cursor to B of "Budget
Variances", hold down the <CTRL> key and press PB(^PB.)
Move the cursor to the space after "Budget Variances," use
^PB again. You will see:

    ^BBudget Variances^B

3. To delete a sentence, you must first block it. Move the cursor to the beginning of the last sentence, hold down the <CTRL> key and press KB(^KB) to specify the beginning of the block operation. Move the cursor to the end of the sentence, hold down the <CTRL> key and press KK(^KK) to specify the end of the blocking operation.

4. Use ^KY to delete the sentence.

5. Save and print the document.

PART C

Two more changes are needed to complete the memorandum.

1. Open the document named **MEMO**.

2. Boldface the first sentence in the document to make it stand out. Move the cursor to the beginning of the first sentence, hold down the <CTRL> key and press PB(^PB.) Move the cursor to the end of the sentence, use ^PB again.

3. To underline the word "exceeded" in the first paragraph, use ^PS.

4. Save and print the revised document.

EXERCISE 4

Business Terms

Commands used: OPENING MENU:

L -- change logged disk drive
D -- open a document file
P -- print a document

MAIN MENU:

<CTRL> S -- move cursor one
              character to the left
<CTRL> D -- move cursor one
              character to the right
<CTRL> A -- move cursor one word
              to the left
<CTRL> F -- move cursor one word
              to the right
<CTRL> E -- move cursor up one
              line
<CTRL> V -- move cursor down one
              line
<CTRL> G -- delete the character
              that the cursor is
              sitting on
<CTRL> N -- insert a line

BLOCK MENU:
<CTRL> K to bring up Block Menu

<CTRL> KD -- save the document and
               return to the Opening
               Menu
<CTRL> KB -- begin block operations
<CTRL> KK -- end block operations
<CTRL> KY -- delete blocked text

PRINT MENU:
<CTRL> P to bring up Print Menu

<CTRL> PB -- boldface printing
<CTRL> PS -- underline text

NOTE: <CTRL> may be represented by the symbol ^. For
      example: ^N.

Level of Difficulty: [2]

Purpose: Temporary margin settings are
highlighted in this exercise.

PROBLEM:

You have been asked to keyboard a list of business terms for
an upcoming seminar. The list is displayed in FIGURE 4.1.

ANALYSIS:

Your supervisor has asked you to boldface the terms and
indent the definitions. WordStar has a special feature that
allows the user to set up a "hanging indent." After ^OG is
pressed, the left margin is set at the first tab stop and
the rest of the paragraph will be indented. To restore the
original left margin setting, press the RETURN or ENTER key.
To type up terms exactly as shown in FIGURE 4.1, you may
institute the ^OG command only after your cursor has past
the first tab stop on the first line of each paragraph.

DEVELOPMENT:

PART A

1.   Open a new document named **LIST**.

2.   Type the terms and definitions as shown in FIGURE 4.1
below.

3.   Boldface all the terms using ^PB.

4.   After keyboarding the terms and the two dashes (--),
press ^OG to move the left margin to the first tab stop and
keyboard remaining lines of the paragraph.

5.   Make sure that you place one blank line between each
paragraph.

6.   Save the document.

7.   Print the document.

Accommodation Paper--A promissory note that has been signed
on the back in order to help a person with weak credit
obtain a loan. The accommodation endorser is not
liable unless the maker defaults on his obligation.

Accountability--The ultimate responsibility for proper completion of a task even if the task has been delegated to a subordinate.

Accounts Payable--A current liability representing the amount owed by an individual or a business to a creditor for merchandise or services purchased on open account or short-term credit.

Accounts Receivable--The amounts owed a business enterprise for merchandise bought on open account without the giving of a note or other evidence of debt.

Accrued Expense--An account on an income statement indicating an obligation which has been contracted but not yet paid.

Accrued Income--An account on an income statement indicating earnings which have not yet been received.

Bill of Materials--A list of every kind of raw material or semifinished goods needed for a production run specifying the quantity needed.

Business Law--A body of law that applies specifically to the conduct of business activities.

C.O.D.--Cash On Delivery. Collection of a specific amount from the buyer as the services are rendered or the goods are delivered.

Commodity Rate--A reduced rate offered by railroads for certain basic goods that are shipped from and to stations of origin and destination.

Consumer Finance--The granting of credit to consumers by retailers, banks, and other lending agencies.

Debt Financing--Funds raised by a business through borrowing or the sale of bonds.

Equity Financing--Funds raised by a business by selling ownership shares.

FOB Shipping Point--Free on board from the shipping point whereby the buyer pays for the transportation costs except for loading the goods at the seller's location.

FOB Destination--Free on board to destination whereby the
seller pays for the transportation costs up to
unloading the goods at the buyer's location.

FIGURE 4.1

PART B

While proofreading the printout, you noticed the last two
paragraphs are not in alphabetical order. Use the block
commands to correct it.

1. Open the document named **LIST**.

2. Use ^KB and ^KK to highlight the last paragraph.

3. Use ^KV to move the highlighted paragraph.

4. Save and print the document.

PART C

The manager forgot to specify margin settings. Adjust the
left margin to 5 and the right margin to 60. Normally, when
changing margin settings you simply move the cursor to the
beginning of each paragraph and use ^B. It will be more
complex to format the document using the new margin settings
since you have already established temporary margin
settings.

1. Open the document called **LIST**.

2. Set the margins to 5 and 60.

3. Move the cursor to the beginning of the first paragraph,
make sure INSERT is ON. Press the <TAB> key once to move
this line to the new left margin.

4. Turn off the INSERT mode using ^V. Press the <TAB> once
to move the cursor to the second tab setting.

5. Use ^OG to set a temporary margin. Press ^B to format
the rest of the paragraph.

6. Repeat steps 3-5 for the rest of the text.

7. Save and print the document.

EXERCISE 5

Newsletter

Commands used: OPENING MENU:

L -- change logged disk drive
D -- open a document file
P -- print a document
O -- copy a file

MAIN MENU:

<CTRL> S -- move cursor one
            character to the left
<CTRL> D - move cursor one
            character to the right
<CTRL> A -- move cursor one word
            to the left
<CTRL> F -- move cursor one word
            to the right
<CTRL> E -- move cursor up one
            line
<CTRL> V -- move cursor down one
            line
<CTRL> G -- delete the character
            that the cursor is
            sitting on
<CTRL> N -- insert a line
<CTRL> B -- reform text

BLOCK MENU:
<CTRL> K to bring up Block Menu

<CTRL> KD -- save the document and
            return to the opening
            menu
<CTRL> KS -- save the document and
            return to Main Menu
<CTRL> KQ -- abandon the editing
            version of the
            document only, this
            command does not
            erase the saved
            document.
<CTRL> KB -- begin block operations
<CTRL> KK -- end block operations
<CTRL> KY -- delete blocked text
<CTRL> KV -- move blocked text
<CTRL> KN -- turn on/off column
            mode

ONSCREEN MENU:
<CTRL> O to bring up Onscreen Menu

<CTRL> OR -- change right margin

NOTE: <CTRL> may be represented by the symbol ^. For
      example: ^N

Level of difficulty: [3]

            Purpose: The multiple column facilities of
                           WordStar are demonstrated in this
                           exercise.

PROBLEM:

You work for Spokane Public Radio (KPBX FM 91.) Part of
your job requires the preparation of a newsletter each
month. For the month of November, you have received an
interview (as shown in FIGURE 5.1 on page 22-25) from the
National Public Radio Network. You have been requested to
convert this interview into a newsletter.

ANALYSIS:

WordStar has a **Column Mode** that allows the user to produce
multiple-column text. To do so, you have to make some
decisions on the width of the newsletter and the number of
columns. If you are using standard stationery (8 1/2" x
11"), a two-column newsletter style will fit nicely.
WordStar's default settings are 1 for the left margin and 65
for the right margin. This provides one-inch margins on
both the left and right sides. In other words, there is
room for 65 characters on each line. With 5 spaces between
the two columns, the first column would start at 1, the
second column would start at 36. Each column takes up 30
characters:

        Column one: 1-30 (left margin 1, right margin 30)
        Column two:36-65 (left margin 36, right margin 65)

    |------------------------| |------------------------|
            Column One   Column Two

There are eight steps to create a two-column newsletter:

Step 1: Type the text using the default margin settings
        (1-65).

Step 2: Proofread and save the text.

Step 3: Copy the text using another file name to presecure the text in a backup file.

Step 4: Change the right margin to 30.

Step 5: Format all the text into one narrow column. (This is actually the first column of the two-column text.)

Step 6: Save the text.

Step 7: Determine the total number of text lines in the narrow format(1-30) by looking at the status line on the top of the screen. (For instance, if it indicates page 4, line 18, with 55 lines each page, total number of lines would be 183 (55 lines * 3 = 165 lines, 165 + 18 = 183 lines).

Step 8: Divide the total number of lines by 2 and move second half of the text to the second column.

DEVELOPMENT:

Part A

1. Open a document named **NEWS**.

2. Enter the text as shown in FIGURE 5.1 on pages 22-25.

3. Proofread the text and save it using ^KD.

4. From the Opening Menu, use O to copy a file.

5. When you see the message "Enter the name of the file to copy from:", enter: **NEWS**.

6. When you see the message "Enter the name of the file to copy to:", enter: **NEWS1**.

7. Open the document named **NEWS1**.

8. Use ^OR to set the right margin to 30.

9. Move the cursor to the beginning of the text.

10. Use ^B to format the first paragraph. If you are asked to enter hyphens(-), just use ^B again to ignore the request. Repeat this procedure to format the rest of the paragraphs.

11. Save the text using ^KS. At this point, you have two files with the same text but different formats: the file named **NEWS1** contains text in a narrow column format, the file **NEWS** contains text with the default margin settings.

12. Determine the total number of lines the text contains. If it is an even number, divide by 2 and add 1. The sum tells you the beginning line number of the text to be moved to the second column. If the total number of lines is an odd number, divide by 2 and add 2.

13. With INSERT ON, move the cursor to the beginning of the text to be moved to the second column. Use ^KB to specify the beginning of the block operation. Move the cursor to the bottom of the text, use the space bar to position the cursor one space to the right of the rightmost position of the text. Use ^KK to specify the end of the block operation. Notice that the second half of the text is now highlighted.

14. Set the right margin back to 65.

15. Press ^K to look at the **Block Menu**, the menu shows:

> **N   Column off(on)**

16. To turn on the column mode, just press **N**.

17. Move the cursor to the last character of page one, line one.

18. Press the space bar five times to leave five spaces between the two columns.

19. Use ^KV to move the blocked text to the second column.

20. If the text was moved without disaster, congratulations! Save and print the text. If the text looks funny, use ^KQ to abandon the file. Open the file named NEWS and repeat steps 13-19.

FIGURE 5.1

MOST OFTEN ASKED QUESTIONS ABOUT "A PRAIRIE HOME COMPANION"

Q. How did you come to start the show?

A. In 1974, I was trying to support a family by free-lance writing, and beyond the difficulty of selling enough fiction to put food on the table and clothes on our backs, I had another problem that is common among writers and that was

(continued)

stupor. You can sit in an empty room and look at blank
paper for only so long each day for seven days a week before
your eyes glaze over and your mind turns to lemon meringue.
Other writers learn to take up carpentry or gardening or
golf. I took up this show as my recreation, and it was good
for my disposition. You get tired of the empty room, you
look forward to going on a stage and larking around with
musicians, then you are good and glad to get back to the
empty room. Writing keeps you honest, performing keeps you
sane.

Q. How did you come up with Lake Wobegon?

A. I figured that if I was going to do anything well on the
show, it would probably be comedy. My singing voice then was
not even as good as it is now, and after eight years it
still isn't a voice you'd want to base a career on. I
wasn't much good at comedy either, at least not the zippy
stand-up monologue that we associate with variety shows, but
I figured that comedy at least is a form of writing so I
would stand a chance. Over the first couple years, failure
at stand-up comedy drove me towards storytelling. I started
out telling true stories from my childhood, dressed up as
fiction, and then discovered Lake Wobegon as a place to set
them so as to put more distance between them and the
innocent persons I was talking about.

Q. Is there really a Lake Wobegon? Are any of the things
you mention on the show real such as Powdermilk Biscuits,
Bob Bank, Bertha's Kitty Boutique, the Fearmonger's Shoppe?

A. I don't mean to be cute when I say that this is not an
easy yes-or-no question. No, there is no town in Minnesota
named Lake Wobegon that I could show you, at least I am not
aware of one. But I would also have a hard time showing you
the Ninth Federal Reserve District, the Archdiocese of St.
Paul and Minneapolis, the Big Ten, or the upper middle
class. Most people deal very comfortably with abstractions
much more far-fetched than Lake Wobegon, e.g. the Moral
Majority, secular humanists, Hollywood, etc. Compared to
any of those, Lake Wobegon is as real as my hands on this
typewriter and sometimes more real than that. I once
dreamed that I drove over a hill in central Minnesota and
found it. In the dream, they weren't particularly happy to
see me but they managed to be fairly polite. I was invited
to someone's house for supper and then I woke up.

Q. Do a lot people assume Lake Wobegon is a real place?

A. Some do, who then ask us about it and find out that it
may not be real. I imagine there are other listeners who
know it is real and so don't bother to ask. Maybe they are

FIGURE 5.1 (continued)

up there right now, sitting around in the Chatterbox Cafe, drinking coffee, and thinking, "I could have described this place a lot better than he does."

Q. The greetings you read on the air--are those real or made-up?

A. Real, every single one. We get a couple hundred or so messages every week and try to read about seventy or eighty on the air. They are mostly chosen at random, though I do give preference to funny messages, to happy birthdays to very old people, and to serious messages such as "I'll be on the flight 79 at 5:20 p.m. Sunday--not flight 151 as I told you in the letter." That's the sort of message public radio has an obligation to carry.

Q. How do you select performers for the show?

A. Some are old regulars, like Butch Thompson--I don't remember ever selecting Butch, he seems to have always been there at the piano--and others are people I've admired on records, such as The Boys of the Lough, Helen Schneyer, Claudia Schmidt, Jean Redpath, Queen Ida, Bill Stained, so when they come through Minnesota we grab them. And a few are people who sent us tapes of themselves, we liked what we heard, we had room for them, and we booked them. Nothing mysterious about it.

Q. Why did you get into radio if you are as shy as you claim to be?

A. I needed a part-time job to pay for tuition at the University of Minnesota. I was a parking lot attendant from 1960-62, dropped out for a year because I was broke, and in the fall of 1963, saw an ad offering a job announcing at the University radio station for $1.85 an hour, fifty cents more than I had gotten for parking cars and the radio job was indoors. I think I was the only person to apply for it. All the bright creative people were going into television then. I like radio just fine, even though I was so shy I could hardly bear to be looked at when I was on the air. In time, I learned that the engineers looking at me from the control room didn't really care what I was saying, they only watched out of habit. Even a shy person learns to bear up under pressure when money is at stake. At first, it is agony to press the microphone switch and say, "You're tuned to KUOM 770, the radio voice of the University of Minnesota. It's ten-thirty, and time for Highlights in Homemaking." Gradually, you learn to do this with a high sense of style, making your voice deep and vaguely British. Then gradually

FIGURE 5.1 (continued)

you learn to let yourself talk somewhat naturally. And from there, you just keep digging potatoes and hope for the best.

Q. Why don't you give your name on the air?

A. A vestige of modesty, I guess, and also I don't seem to be able to pronounce it very well. I give it to people over the phone and they always say, "What? Could you spell that?" So I just don't bother with it on the air. It's unreasonable not to, but everyone is entitled to be unreasonable once in a while.

FIGURE 5.1 (continued)

Reprinted with permission from a February 1986 Minnesota Public Radio Interview, "12 Questions Most Asked About 'Prairie Home Companion'." "Prairie Home Companion" is broadcast weekly by American Public Radio.

Part B

Your boss wants you to produce a three-column newsletter and see which style looks better for this document.

1. Copy the document **NEWS** to **NEWS2**.

2. Open the document named **NEWS2**.

3. Allow 4 spaces between columns, each column will be 19 characters in width:

> Column one: 1-19
> Column two: 24-42
> Column three: 47-65

4. Change the right margin to 19.

5. Format the entire text.

6. Divide the number of text lines by 3, if there is a remainder, add 2. Without a remainder, add 1. The resulting number will be the beginning line of text to be moved out of the first column.

7. Block the text to be moved out of the first column.

8. Change the right margin to 42.

9. Make sure the column mode is On.

10. Move the cursor to the beginning of the second column.

11. Move the blocked text.

12. Now the text is in two columns, the second column has twice as much text as the first column. Use ^KS to save the text.

13. Move the second half of the text in column two to column three.

14. Save the text.

15. Print the three-column newsletter.

EXERCISE 6

Lengthy Document

Commands used: OPENING MENU:

L -- change logged disk drive
D -- open a document file
P -- print a document

MAIN MENU:

<CTRL> S -- move cursor one
            character to the left
<CTRL> D -- move cursor one
            character to the right
<CTRL> A -- move cursor one word
            to the left
<CTRL> F -- move cursor one word
            to the right
<CTRL> E -- move cursor up one
            line
<CTRL> V -- move cursor down one
            line
<CTRL> G -- delete the character
            that the cursor is
            sitting on
<CTRL> N -- insert a line
<CTRL> Y -- delete a line

PRINT MENU:
<CTRL> P to bring up Print Menu

<CTRL> PB -- boldface printing
<CTRL> PS -- underline text

BLOCK MENU:
<CTRL> K to bring up Block Menu

<CTRL> KD -- save document and
             return to Opening Menu
<CTRL> KS -- save document and
             return to Main Menu

NOTE: <CTRL> may be rpresented by the symbol ^. For
      example: ^N

DOT COMMANDS:
Commands start with a period and
are always entered at the very
beginning of the document.

.HE text -- place the header text
            at the top of each page

.FO text -- place the footer text
            at the bottom of each
            page

.OP -- omit page-numbering

Level of difficulty: [2]

Purpose: WordStar provides an array of
         powerful dot commands. This
         exercise features the header,
         footer, and page length dot
         commands.

PROBLEM:

You are using WordStar to write a book on the database
software dBase III. The first chapter has been
completed(see FIGURE 6.1 on pages 29-32.) Even with this
small amount of text, you have already come to realization
that both page-numbering and titling are crucial factors.
Finding a particular page or subject would be greatly
facilitated by the additions of page numbers and chapter
titles.

ANALYSIS:

You would like to have a header at the top of each page
without entering it manually. WordStar allows the user to
do this with dot commands. The dot command ".HE text" will
place one line of text at the top of each page of your
document. The dot command ".FO text" will place one line of
text at the bottom of every page. In order for WordStar to
recognize these dot commands, they must appear at the
beginning of the document.

DEVELOPMENT

Part A

1. Open a new document named **BOOK.**

2. Keyboard: **.he Introduction to dBase III.**

3. Keyboard the text as shown in FIGURE 6.1 on pages 29-32.

4. Save the text.

5. Print the text.

6. If the header is printed incorrectly, check to make sure there is no space before the dot command.

FIGURE 6.1

What is a Database?

A database is nothing more than a collection of related facts. The filing cabinet found in any office is really a database. The telephone directory laying near your phone is also a database. There is nothing mysterious or mystic about databases and from the above examples it is obvious that a database need not reside in a computer. However, computer databases do offer some distinct advantages over manual systems. For instance, the file folders in an office filing cabinet are usually ordered alphabetically. To manually reorder or **sort** these same folders on some other basis, say Zip Code, involves an enormous effort. With a computer, the task is quite simple. Also, locating or **searching** out a specific folder in a filing cabinet is a time-consuming process when compared to searching with a computer.

This text will show you how to use dBase III to sort and search a database. It will teach you to create, add to, and correct your database. Before you create one, you need to understand how computer databases are structured.

What is the structure of a Database?

While an office filing cabinet is made up of folders, a computerized database is made up of **records**. Imagine a filing cabinet filled with hundreds of folders. Each folder contains a line for a client's (1)Name, (2)Address, (3)City, State, Zip Code, and (4)Telephone Number. (See Example 1.)

```
----------------------------------------------
|      (1)   John Doe                        |
|      (2)   East 2217 Bismark               |
|      (3)   Spokane, WA  99207              |
|      (4)   487-3333                        |
|                                            |
----------------------------------------------
```
Example 1

(continued)

This is the same kind of information a computer
database might contain. However, in a computer, client data
is stored in a record instead of a folder. In addition,
each line of information is referred to as a **field** and must
be given a name. The fields in a computerized database are
very rigid in structure. Besides naming each line, you must
also tell the computer how long the largest field entry will
be and what kind of data will be entered in the field (more
on the last subject later).

dBase III has several limits for records and fields:

254 characters per field
128 fields per record
4000 characters total per record

Even though the above are limits, it is advisable to keep
the number of fields and their length to a minimum to
conserve storage space. This requires careful planning.
A complete assessment of information needs should be made
before a system is created. Future users of the database
should be questioned to determine their information
expectations concerning the nature of the information they
hope to get from the system. Based on this assessment, the
structure of the database should be designed to include
fields to hold the data necessary for answering user's
requests. For example, look back at Example 1. You will
notice both the first and last name are included on the same
line. If both are entered in the same field in a database,
the computer is unable to sort the file based on just the
last name. This is because the computer needs a separate
and **unique** field to sort on. The same sorting problem would
arise in conjunction with the City, State, and Zip Code
line. To sort on Zip Code the data must be stored in its
own unique field. Example 2 depicts a scheme which would
allow sorting based on any of the individual fields.

```
 --------------------------------------------------------
|                                                        |
|          FNAME: John                                   |
|          LNAME: Doe                                    |
|          ADDRESS: East 2217 Bismark                    |
|          CITY: Spokane                                 |
|          STATE: WA                                     |
|          ZIP: 99207                                    |
|          PHONE:  487-3333                              |
|                                                        |
 --------------------------------------------------------
```
                          Example 2
FIGURE 6.1 (continued)

(Notice the field names to the left of the actual data. When entering data, dBase III will also display the chosen field names left of the data entry spaces.) The moral of this story is to be sure to create unique fields for any data you may wish to sort on.

One final point on structure. Fields may contain various types of data. You need to tell the computer in advance what type of data a particular field will hold. dBase III has five allowable field types:

1. C character
2. N numeric
3. D date
4. M memo
5. L logical

Character Fields may consist of any combination of letters, numbers, and/or special ASCII characters.

Numeric Fields store numbers which are intended for computations.

Date Fields are designed specifically to hold a single date in the form of MM/DD/YY where MM=month, DD=day, and YY=year. The field length is automatically set to 8 characters.

Memo Fields are like character fields except they are designed to store blocks of data. They are very useful for storing up to 4000 characters of text with each record.

Logical Fields are only one character in length and contain either a "T" for **True** or "F" for **False**. Until a T is entered in this field, it will display an F.

You will soon use all of the above field types to build your first Data Base. But once you have created a Data Base, what can you do with it?

What is the function of a Database?

There are five basic functions performed by computerized database systems:

1. Entry
2. Editing
3. Sorting

FIGURE 6.1 (continued)

4. Searching
5. Reporting

dBase III has a built-in data entry program which makes adding records easy. It also has an edit program for updating or correcting records. Searching and sorting are accomplished by the use of several key words and expressions. dBase III provides two reporting programs for both column type reports and mail labels.

FIGURE 6.1 (continued)

Part B

WordStar prints page numbers at the bottom of each page. You want to insert the identifying word "Page" to the left of the page numbers.

1. Open the document named **BOOK.**

2. Insert a blank line between the heading and the text.

3. Type: **.fo - Page # -** to create a footing. To center the footing, enter 27 blank spaces after "**.fo.**"

4. Save and print the document.

Part C

After you look at the printout from Part B, you decided to combine the page-numbering with the heading.

1. Open the document named **BOOK.**

2. Delete the footing line using ^Y (hold down <CTRL> key and press Y.)

3. Change the heading line to the following:

   .he Introduction to dBase III -----------------Page #

4. Save and print the text.

Part D

Notice that the printout from Part C has two page numbers;
one at the top and the other at the bottom. The bottom one
comes with WordStar's default settings. You can issue a dot
command to omit the bottom page-numberings.

1. Open the document named **BOOK**.

2. Insert a blank line between the heading and the text.

3. Type: **.op**.

4. Save and print the document.

EXERCISE 7

Create Mailing Labels

Commands used: OPENING MENU

        L -- change logged disk drive
        D -- open a document file
        N -- open a non-document file
        M -- mailmerge

        BLOCK MENU:
        <CTRL> K to bring up Block Menu

        <CTRL> KD -- save the document and
                      return to Opening Menu

NOTE: <CTRL> may be represented by the symbol ^. For
     example: ^N.

        DOT COMMANDS:
        Commands start with a period and
        are always entered at the very
        beginning of the document.

        .op -- omit page-numbering
        .pl -- page length
        .mt -- top margin
        .mb -- bottom margin
        .df -- data file
        .rv -- record variables
        .. -- ignore this line

Level of difficulty: [3] [This exercise requires the
                      mailmerge option.]

       Purpose: This exercise demonstrates
                 WordStar's ability to create
                 mailing labels from a non-document
                 data file.

PROBLEM:

The company you work for sends out monthly statements to its
customers. To address envelopes for each statement requires
a great deal of time. Realizing the computer does
repetitive tasks well, you decided to use WordStar to
generate mailing labels.

ANALYSIS:

To print mailing labels, WordStar requires two files: a document file and a non-document file. The document file gives the computer instructions as to which data file to use, what to print, and the size of the mailing labels used. The non-document file is a data file that stores the customers' names and addresses.

In the document file, dot commands are used to specify page length, top & bottom margins, and the data file. Before designing the document file, you have to know the length of the mailing labels, the type of information printed on the labels, and the information in the data file. The standard mailing label is six lines in length. Since only four lines of information will be printed, both the top and bottom margins are set at one.

```
-----------------------------------------------------------------

..              File Name: LABEL
.op             Omit Page-numbering
.pl6            Page Length is 6 lines
.mt1            Top Margin is 1 line
.mb1            Bottom Margin is 1 line
.dfMAIL.DAT     Data File is MAIL.DAT
.rvNUMBER,NAME,COMPANY,ADDRESS1,ADDRESS2
        &NAME&
        &COMPANY&
        &ADDRESS1&
        &ADDRESS2&
..end of file


-----------------------------------------------------------------
```
                        FIGURE 7.1

FIGURE 7.1 illustrates a document file. Notice that this file contains only dot commands. Each command is followed by a line of explanation which is optional.   The first and last lines are special dot commands. They start with two dots(..), which tells the computer to ignore the line and allows the user to write a note for future reference. The dot command **.rv** stands for Record Variables, which tells the computer that every record contains the following variables. To specify the layout of the labels, use an "&" before and after each variable.

There are some basic rules for a non-document data file:

1. From the opening menu, use N to open a non-document file.

2. Begin each record with a record number. Each name and address is considered as a record. Assign record numbers in sequence.

3. Use a comma after record numbers.

4. Separate name, company, street address, and city/state/zip with commas.

5. Use the Return key after each record.;

6. Use double quotation marks before and after categories that contain commas of their own.

7. For each record, all the variables are needed. If a category is unknown, type a blank space followed by a comma.

FIGURE 7.2 shows a non-document file.

```
1,Richard Able,Able & Associates,1102 Cook Street,"Edmond,
OK 34567"
2,Bob Wiley,Acme TV,123 W. First Ave.,"San Jose, CA 83721"
3,Donna Reed,Dragon Inc.,E.9203 Wellesley,"Sand Point, ID
19203"
4,Larry Olson, ,N.19207 Hamilton,"Los Angelos, CA 99687"
5,Debbie Walter, ,W.403 Nevada,"Eugene, OR 20345"
```

FIGURE 7.2

DEVELOPMENT:

Part A

1. Use N from Opening Menu to create a non-document file named **MAIL.DAT**.

2. Enter records from FIGURE 7.2 exactly as shown.

3. Save the data file.

4. Use D from Opening Menu to open a document file named **LABEL**.

5. Enter Figure 7.1 on page 35 exactly as shown.

6. Save the document.

7. Make sure the printer and labels are ready. At the Opening Menu, select **M** for mailmerge.

8. Enter **LABEL** as the name of the document file to
mailmerge. At this point, WordStar loads up the document
file named **LABEL** and in this file, the dot command **.df**
identifies the data file to be used.

9. Press the **<ESC>** key to begin printing.

10. If the labels were printed incorrectly, check the
following:

    A. If the mailing labels look like Figure 7.3, check
    the document file named **LABEL** and make sure that
    .dfMAIL.DAT command is present.

        &NAME&
        &COMPANY&
        &ADDRESS1&
        &ADDRESS2&

FIGURE 7.3

    B. Make sure the non-document data file was named
    correctly.

    C. If the printer rolls up one full page after each
    label is printed, check the dot command that specifies
    the page length in the document file named **LABEL**.

    D. If the record number is printed on the labels, check
    the dot command that specifies category names. It
    should read:

      .rvNUMBER,NAME,COMPANY,ADDRESS1,ADDRESS2

    E. If mailing labels #4 and #5 were printed
    incorrectly, check record #4 and #5 of the non-document
    data file named **MAIL.DAT**. Make sure that the blank
    spaces are entered for customers without company name.

Part B

1. Open the non-document data file named **MAIL.DAT**.

2. Add the names shown in Figure 7.4.

3. Save the file.

4. Print the mailing labels.

John Presley	Bill Weber
1948 N.W. Blvd	Abacus Accounting
New York, NY 10294	S. 940 Havana
	High Land, AK 95067
Edward Black	Rick Schmidt
E. 25345 Sprague	Houston Cleaning
Juneau, AK 93049	N. 234 1234th Ave.
	Houston, TX 38405
Bud Maricle	Stacey Rogers
Utter Cadillac	Computer Services
1527 N.E. Dr.	W. 1723 Indiana
Moses Lake, WA 99230	Albany, NY 30945
Pauline Crull	Sally Ralph
San Diego Auto	Super Savings Bank
N. 284 Superior	N. 28506 384th Ave.
Helena, MT 68963	Des Moines, IO 27495

FIGURE 7.4

Part C

The company is going to send out Christmas cards to its
customers. The envelopes included with the Christmas cards
are green. The white mailing labels look inappropriate on
the green envelopes, so you decide to alter the document
file to print on envelopes instead of mailing labels.

1. Open the document named **LABEL**.

2. Change the page length, top margin, and bottom margin.
These parameters depend on envelope size.

3. Since you can only print one envelope at a time, you
need to make some changes to the document file. Insert the
following lines before &NAME&

    ..   **Press <CTRL> PC to insert ^C on the next line**
    ^C   **Wait for the next envelope**

4. Replace the last line with the following:

    .pa   Roll envelope out of the printer

5. Save the document. It should look like Figure 7.5.

6. Insert an envelope in the printer.

7.   Press **M** for mailmerge.

8.   After the envelope is printed, insert another envelope
in the printer. Repeat this until all records in the data
file are printed.

```
..                 File Name: LABEL
.op                Omit Page-numbering
.pl6               Page Length is 6 lines
.mt1               Top Margin is 1 line
.mb                Bottom Margin is 1 line
.dfMAIL.DAT        Data File is MAIL.DAT
.rvNUMBER,NAME,COMPANY,ADDRESS1,ADDRESS2
..                 Press <CTRL> PC to insert ^C on the next line
^C                 Wait for the next envelope
        &NAME&
        &COMPANY&
        &ADDRESS1&
        &ADDRESS2&
.pa                Roll envelope out of the printer
```

                         FIGURE 7.5